Then and Now

The Life of Percy Manning

by Percy Manning

Edited by Geoff Wright

All about life in the last century until the present time, but mainly about various forms of transport and how it has improved.
As you read, you will be able to decide:
'Were they Good Old Days, or not?'

Percy Manning

Then and Now: The Life of Percy Manning
by Percy Manning

(Edited by Geoff Wright)

Published by Carnegie Press, 18 Maynard Street, Preston PR2 2AL.
Typeset in 9½pt Times and Caslon Medium by Carnegie Press.
Printed by T. Snape & Co. Ltd., Boltons Court, Preston

First edition, November 1989

ISBN 0 948789 45 X

Contents

All profits from the sale of this book will be used by Southport General Hospital for the purchase of equipment for the cure of forms of cancer.

By buying this book you will be helping in the fight against cancer.

Foreword

CANCER is one of the last great medical scourges. One person in three in the U.K. is affected at some time. One in five dies from it. But cancer can be beaten. Every year 75,000 people are treated successfully in this country and advances in some areas have been dramatic. Twenty years ago, for example, a diagnosis of Hodgkin's Disease in a young person was virtually a death sentence. Today, nine out of ten recover.

The main reason for writing this book is to raise money for cancer research. In recent years, I have made four full-size street organs which are displayed and operated at functions by members of the Imperial Cancer Research Fund Committees who have collected many thousands of pounds.

I have also made nearly one hundred rocking horses, plant stands and bird feeding tables, which have been sold or raffled.

Since my dear wife passed away seven years ago through cancer, I have devoted my time to making things for the Imperial Cancer Reseach Fund. It gives me great pleasure to know that my efforts have contributed towards giving cancer sufferers the help and hope that my late wife possibly did not have.

I am now aged 90 myself and looking forward to the day when my book will be on sale, as the profits will be used to contribute to some large piece of medical equipment before I go to the great beyond.

Percy Manning

Chapter One

The Mannings of Castle Acre

MY FATHER was born in a little village with a long and proud history called Castle Acre, in Norfolk. Many changes have taken place there over the years and, recently, a census showed that the population was increasing more rapidly than in the country as a whole. This has brought about many alterations to the landscape, the buildings and, of course, the way of life.

Village developments have sometimes been well planned but invariably far from simple. Traditional cottages have become trendy, with carriage lamps and old tumble wheels and some of the great barns are now luxury homes. There are many new roads and some of the towns and villages are now by-passed and, of course, the few railway lines that are left are always under threat of closure. No doubt these are national trends and, in a sense, Norfolk has been relatively fortunate in that many have arrived late there.

Nevertheless, there are still 659 magnificent medieval churches to be seen in Norfolk, even if some of them are not worshipped in any more. There are many historic houses maintained by the National Trust and marshes and shores with their numerous rare birds. Norfolk, in spite of all its changes, still has a character all of its own. The villages and their sites belong to time immemorial. Each human settlement has a long history, many of which can be traced back into the Dark Ages.

One brief mention may be made of the pre-Roman Iron Age village of West Harling, where a circular structure was discovered which had been a home to more than one family. It belongs to the milennium before the arrival of the first Anglo-Saxon settlers in England. It and similar places have left only the slightest traces and, excepting the walls of Roman towns, the only visible remains in Norfolk are those of the 9th century and beyond.

Castle Acre boasts many historical remains. Apart from the ruins of a Cluniac Priory, it has perhaps the best set of castle earthworks in the country. Covering fifteen acres, they are dominated by a mound of earth, a 'motte' of great height of over thirty metres from the bottom of the ditch to the top. The earthworks encompass the whole village.

Castle Acre Church is exceptional in the area, as it is built of stone rarely used in churches out of town. It was built by William d'Albini who died in 1176. The west front of St. Lawrence's Church has Norman decoration. The tower, too, is Norman, although the top was restored in 1844. The Manning family supplied four successive rectors in the parish from 1778 to 1916, including a noted local historian and another of the family, Thomas Manning, was the first Englishman to reach Lhasa. I intend to find out whether we are related to any other branch of the Manning dynasty in the area.

I visited Castle Acre in 1920 while I was in the Army. Because by father's family had lived there, I was keen to see the old place. My grandfather had owned the village bakery, although originally he had been the village carpenter. While I was looking around the village, I came across some elderly men sitting on a form and was asking them something, when one of them said:

'You've been here before, haven't you?'.

'No,' I said.

But he persisted, 'I'm sure you have'.

Despite my further denials, he asked by name and, on hearing it, quickly responded, 'Ah yes, I knew your father very well. How is he?'

I believe that my grandfather owned quite a lot of property in and around Castle Acre. He turned into an alcoholic, however, and lost most of his money. He turned teetotal almost overnight, the change apparently disagreed with him and he did not live very long after!

My mother was born in King's Lynn. She had three sisters and a brother. Her father was a policeman and they lived in a little terraced house in Kepple Street. I went down there one time because I had remembered staying there with my mother, but it has since been demolished. I have heard my mother say that whenever anybody came begging at the door and their parents were out, they would carry one of their father's helmets to the door, pretending to clean it and, of course, whoever was there would assume the policeman to be inside and soon beat a hasty retreat.

My mother served her time as a milliner. One of my aunts served her time as a dressmaker and my uncle was a joiner. My uncle was a very good swimmer and diver and I am told that once he dived off one of the high pinnacles on the railway bridge across the Ouse, as a result of which he was deafened for life.

King's Lynn, where my mother grew up, was a very busy port in those days. Evidence of its former commercial success can still be seen readily around the port and in the market place. My mother would sometimes go on a collier which plied from Newcastle to King's Lynn as my grandfather was a friend of the captain. He would invite my mother to go with him and she looked upon it as a great adventure. My mother would cook the meals for the crew on the boat, but life on a collier was no picnic, what with all the coal dust and the rough weather in the North Sea. Nevertheless, my mother was a great adventurer.

Chapter Two

Growing up in Southport

MY FATHER and mother used to holiday occasionally in Lancashire. I remember once when they were being visited by her sister and an uncle. They took a boat from Southport Pier one morning. The sea was very rough and when they arrived in Blackpool, my uncle and his wife decided to come back to Southport on the train instead of hazarding the rough sea crossing again. My mother and father were made of sterner stuff, however, and they came home by boat. They regretted their bravery, for the sea was so rough that they had to batten the passengers down in the saloon. The waves washed over the boat and they had a very hazardous disembarkment at Southport Pier. Mother, of course, was used to the sea from her trips aboard the collier to Newcastle but father was less well prepared.

My uncle was a signalman and his box was on the bridge over the River Ouse. One time, he took me up to spend an hour or so with him in the signal box. During my stay, one of the fiercest thunderstorms I can remember broke out. Suddenly lightning struck the box and flashed across all the levers. All the bells started ringing and, being very young, I was terrified. I hid under the desk until it was all over and I asked him if this sort of thing was usual, to which he replied in the negative, much to my relief, but added that other mishaps did indeed occur, such as the odd derailing of trains, a catastrophe about which he was reasonably phlegmatic, saying simply, "Oh yes, it cannot be helped sometimes."

My grandfather had a beautiful allotment in Norfolk. He used to graft all his own roses and he grew all his own vegetables. I remember distinctly that he grew no fewer than three sorts of currants - white, red and black; I was amazed that there existed such a thing as white currants. He also grew delicious dessert-type gooseberries. There was never a blade of grass or a weed of any sort on his allotment. I suppose that both my father and I inherited this love of gardening. Certainly, we later both kept allotments close to each other. I always remember one time, long ago, when I was talking to father in the allotment. He suddenly announced that he was fed up of there being no means of getting water nearby and that he intended to dig a well. I took little notice and returned to my own allotment to continue work. After a while I looked along the line but could not see father. I thought that perhaps I should go along and check that everything was alright, since I had not seen him go past me.

As I approached his allotment all I could see were shovels full of soil coming out of the ground. He had dug the hole and he was almost out of sight. The next day he went to the local scrapyard and bought a metal cylinder which was about seven or eight feet long and about three feet in diameter. He had this delivered to the allotment and it was unloaded off the roadway but he managed to roll it up towards the hole. He got back into the hole and started digging again and, as he was digging the soil out the cylinder sank further down until eventually he was in so much water that he couldn't stand up without it going over the top of his wellies. He then put a top on the well and bought an old pump from the marine store and fitted leather washers onto it. He was the envy of the allotments because he was the only one who had water. He was a grand old chap and lived to be 93, happy to the last.

My father got a job as an apprentice with the local coach builder and wheelwright. It was very hard work, consisting mainly of sawing up logs by hand over a saw pit. Inevitably, the apprentice was put down the hole to hold one end of the huge saw while the experienced man wielded the other end in the relative luxury of the open air. The planks, which would have taken ages to cut, were left for around three years to season fully before they were used. Eventually they were cut into various shapes and sizes for cart shafts, felloes for the wheels and all sorts of things.

After a few months, my father saw an advert in one of the trade journals for young men to serve their time as coach and carriage builders on the broad gauge Great Western Railway at Swindon. He applied for the post, got it and moved down to Swindon where he signed an articled apprenticeship on a £5 penalty agreement for a period of five years. The GWR demanded very high levels of quality and my father finished his apprenticeship with high-class finish and craftsmanship. When he returned to King's Lynn he got a job with a local coach builder and he also joined a volunteer band.

A very significant event then followed when my parents were visiting some friends in Liverpool, with whom they had gone to school. They suggested to my parents that this part of the country was much more likeable than where they were at the moment. The idea took hold and, being of an adventurous turn of mind, they decided to make the move.

My father duly got a job as a first-class carriage builder to a firm in Bootle and soon got used to making good-quality carriages for doctors, professional men, lords and ladies, who mostly had high-stepping horses or coach and pairs, together with dapper fitted coachmen, breeches and leather boots. These coachmen, apart from seeing to the horses, had to wash and leather the coaches or traps, no matter what time they came in; otherwise, if it had been raining, the paintwork would invariably be covered in almost immovable spots and specks.

It was at this time that my father became involved with music again. He had been in the old volunteer brass band in King's Lynn and had also helped with the police band as my grandfather was a Sergeant cornet player. However, he joined the Bootle Borough Band as a tenor horn player and made some very good friends there.

One day, my mother and father were out walking in Southport and my father noticed how few coach builders and wheelwrights there appeared to be in Southport. They talked it over and decided to take advantage of the situation. They moved to Southport with the intention of starting their own business.

Always adventurous, he hunted around for some premises to rent to carry on the trades of coach building, wheelwrighting and black-smithing. He was very fortunate in getting a good wheelwright and a blacksmith and two apprentices and soon worked up a good business. The other traders were apparently the instigators of complaints from neighbours, however, and he was given notice to quit.

He found some other suitable premises and had to move the forge and other equipment, benches, etc. Soon he was in production once again, but this time the landlord was very greedy and forced the rents and rates up out of all reason, so my father decided to look around for somewhere to build his own works.

He borrowed some money and bought a pair of houses in Chatham Road with large gardens and good entrances. Plans were passed for a two-storey brick building across the bottom end for woodworking on one half and painting in the other on both floors. The smithy and the shoeing hovel were on the left-hand side and there was room to have a fire for heating the hoops for the wheels. Ultimately, he covered the whole area and made a nice big workshop. After the whole area had been cleared and the rubbish burnt, the footings were dug out. No concrete was used then, just the bricks laid down on the sand. The bricks were delivered in heavily built carts with two 5ft 6ins wheels and heavy shafts hinged so that the load could be tipped when a lever was pulled out and, in fact, they were called kecking carts and pulled by huge shire horses. There were two hinged stands under the shafts to hold the cart upright when the horse was not in the shafts and a permanent short piece of rope on the front end of the cart which the driver used to hitch round a spoke in the wheel. When the horse moved off it pulled the cart up into position as it was far too heavy for one man to pull up. Father bought a lot of timber, windows and doors, etc. from the old Walton Jail and borrowed a horse and a lorry to enable him to bring them back to Southport. Unfortunately the horse died on its second journey, which was rather embarrassing. I do not know how my father compensated for that.

The bricklayer was a middle-aged man and an inveterate tobacco chewer who always had saliva running down his chin. He had a habit of digging you in the ribs with his thumb to emphasise a point and if you were not careful he would knock you off the scaffolding. When the rafters were in position on the walls and the floors, I spotted a long ladder that went up to the apex, so I went up to see what it looked like from up above. I was so frightened when I did look down that I had to call my father to carry me down. When the building was completed, the top space in the roof was used as the upholstery workshop.

My mother would stitch the cushions together, including the piping, which meant four layers of material having to be sewn on an ordinary hand sewing machine and father would stuff them with horse hair which had been pulled from horses tails and manes. We had a special machine called a teasing machine that had a drum which was full of spikes and when the drum was turned it would shred the hair, if it had been used before, to make it fluffy and springy. The first floor on the left was used for coach building and the one on the right was used for painting. The carts were hauled up on heavy wooden channels with a rope around the shafts to hold them level and one around the axle connected to a winch which would be turned by hand.

Father came to be a dab hand at stitching up the polished black leather on the shafts where the harness rubbed along the tapered front ends for about two feet.

The neighbours at the bottom behind the works had always been awkward since the first work started and under the ancient order of lights boarded our windows up, which was indeed a blow, especially in the paint shop. Father could not do anything about it. In fact, the works were nearly burnt down at a later date when a painter, who was using a candle to see the paint around the floorboards in the front of a car, caught the celluloid covering the steering wheel and set it alight which, in turn, set fire to the covering on the ceiling of the paint shop. The fire had to be put out with water, a bit sharpish, as there were no fire extinguishers in those days.

All the machinery was turned by hand so the apprnetices had to take turns. There was a big drilling machine with the fly wheel on top and turning it in a horizontal plane would create such a draft if it was turned too fast.

We would have to make our own drills out of old files and, of course, they only ground their way through the metal using copious doses of old oil. The band saw used for cutting mostly curved shapes had three wheels in order to give a longer throat to enable wider boards to be cut. It had a large fly wheel with a handle and, of course, the apprentices eventually developed big muscles with having to turn it for hours on end. It was a long boring job sharpening and setting blades as the saws were so long.

I think it worth describing how we made cart wheels in those days. The centre, called the nave, was turned from hard wood, some decorative for carriages, etc., and others for wagons and vans, plain and with a nominal sized hole to carry the cast bush. The spokes were eventually made by machine, and shaped eliptically, having a tang on one end shaped rectangular to be let into the mortices or holes in the nave. The other end was left, and the felloes or rim were cut to size for a given diameter of wheel and the number required to enable each felloe to accommodate two spokes.

The nave was marked out and drilled and mortice slots were chiselled out with heavy chisels and a two face hammer, to the required sizes to fit the spokes which were then dipped in red lead paint and driven into the slots. The spokes were then cut to length, which was done with two pieces of wood bolted at one end to swivel, and one part was put into the hole in the nave and the trammel, which it was called, rotated round the outer end of the spokes and marked with a spike. They were then cut to length and shouldered down to fit the holes in the felloes which were clamped together in line and put into a trestle. The positions of the holes were then marked out and centred with a big nail. A large two handled brace and a centre bit usually one inch in diameter were used. This is where I came in and during my two years apprenticeship in the woodwork shop, I was helping Rave one day to hold the brace. Rave held the brace with one hand under his chin and one of my hands and as he chewed tobacco all day his chin bobbed up and down which made me laugh, both of us then turned the brace drilling the holes and it was remarkable how accurate they were considering that they had to have correct angles in three dimensions.

I remember one day I was thinking about something and I was not doing my share of turning and he stopped and gave me a clout on the ear. When I indignantly asked, 'What was that for?', he said, 'Nothing, get on turning.'

Each of the felloes was drilled to accommodate ⅝ dowels to hold them together in a line. Red lead paint was then put on the end of the spokes and the felloes put on one at a time and hammered round in rotation so that the dowels entered the holes.

When they were tight up to the shoulders the spoke ends were split and wooden wedges driven in. These wedges, which apprentices made during slack periods, were made of wood called lance wood using a robust axe that had a bevel on one side only, so a left-hander could not use it. The next job was to chisel out the hole in the nave to suit the cast iron bush, which was roughed out with a sold V-shaped chisel and finished with a big gouge. Of course, it had to be accurate, otherwise the wheel would wobble and to get this accuracy the trammel had to be continually in use and it was amazing how from this crude form of chiselling a craftsman could get the desired result. When the bush was finally hammered in, wedges were driven in all around. Before this was done the blacksmith made wide rings and shrank them on either side on the nave. When the outside of the wheel was planed fairly level the blacksmith came along with another simple tool which was a wheel about 6" in diameter and attached to a handle and run around the wheel counting the number of revolutions and then running along a bar of wrought iron of the right weight and the bar cut to length and then rolled to the right circle, the two ends were then heated and chamfored and welded together in the smithy fire, again a craftman's job. The hoops had then to be heated to expand them and when they were cooled shrunk tight on the wheel. As this meant lighting a big fire in the yard, this was only done when several wheels were ready and often of varying sizes.

In building a fire a record had to be kept as to which wheel was placed on the star, which was spoked and of heavy construction to ensure that the right sized tyre was pulled out of the fire. This was rather a painful operation as the fire was a mass of heat and two men had to rush in with a pair of tongs, grab the tyre and place it on the wheen. Then several water cans would quickly be used to quench the hoop before it burned the wooden wheel. If you missed grabbing the tyre first time, God help you, for the Head Blacksmith would have probably thrown his tongs as you to teach you a lesson. So, next time you see a wooden wheel, you will appreciate the amount of work that went into making it.

I must tell you about Ralph, who for some reason unbeknown to me was known as Rave. Rave was one of the old brigade of wheelwright craftsmen using primitive tools. He originally came from Knotty Ash in Liverpool, Ken Dodd's area. My father borrowed him for a fortnight during a very busy period from another employer and, at the end of the fortnight, my father said:

'Thank you very much, Rave, for helping us out.'

'Don't you like me, boss?', Rave replied.

'I do very much, but I only borrowed you, you know'

'Well, I am not going back,' he said, and he stayed with us for thirty-five years.

Rave used to bring his lunch with him and sit on one of the benches to eat it. Rave had befriended a little stray cat which used to come and visit us on occasions. He would bring a bottle of milk for it and it would come and sit by him on the bench at lunchtime. Unfortunately, one day the cat stepped into some lead paint and he must have licked it off his paws for sadly he died of poisoning. Poor old Rave was in a terrible way, shedding many a tear for his little friend.

Rave was a craftsman and when I was a young boy I used to watch him lining the wheels. He used to put them on a thing called a wheel horse which was simply a post on a base with projected metal about eighteen inches long and which sloped gently upwards so that the wheel would not slip off. He would get a little pot of paint and periodically he would put a little paint on this glass and then get his lining pencil. He would stroke it about in this paint and set it on the wood. He used his finger as a guide to propel the brush along the spoke or felloe. his hands would shake but, nevertheless, the line was always perfectly straight no matter how thin it was – and in some cases the line was very thin, especially on doctors' broughams or Victorias. I remember having a go at this but it was pretty hopeless, apart from running the line parallel to the edge.

The new works in Chatham Road went into production in 1903 and, as there were two forges in the smithy, my father was able to take on another blaksmith and an improver with about three years' experience, together with two apprentices. He soon began to get very busy, with horses of every shape and size to shoe. He had to shoe about 250 horses eventually, together with all the other work such as hooping wheels and making some very fine decorative ironwork for the various vehicles that were now being made.

He also made the springs and axles for vans for butchers, bakers, grocers and governesses, rally cars for pleasure, milk floats, doctors' broughams and landaus, lorries, both heavy and light, and lovely little hand vans which the delivery boys pulled. A horse ambulance was made for the old Birkdale Council in 1904. When it was delivered to the fire station, one apprentice was in the shafts, one pushing behind, and I was sitting up in the driver's seat. About 1912 the wheels were taken from under the body and mounted on a twenty-horsepower Vulcan chassis. Through that, the motor ambulance got to the patient very much more quickly!

The fire engine at this time had a big brass coal-fired boiler and was pulled by two horses which normally stood on the cab rank. The harness was suspended over the pole on the engine for quickness and, when the fire bell rang, one of the cab men ran from the stables enxt door leading the two horses and when in position the harness would be lowered onto them and buckled up.

The firemen were part-time and most of them were tradesmen. When they heard the siren they came as quickly as possible. Inevitably some were delayed and the address of the fire was always chalked up on a board so that latecomers could follow on a bike. The boiler fire was always laid ready to light, which was the job of the first man in to do. When the horse galloped off, one man held for grim death, with one hand holding on, and the other shovelling coal. The boiler also supplied steam to work the pumps if necessary. The fire station adjoined the Corporation yard where the steam rollers were kept, together with the vehicles and horses. The Police Station, Court Rooms (completed in 1891); the old Town Hall (built in 1871 and enlarged in 1906), and the Library (1905), which were demolished in the 1960s, were situated near to Birkdale Railway Station. The Birkdale Corporation was amalgamated with Southport in 1912. The three tramway systems utilised electricity from both towns, before the Corporation held the tram monopoly.

My father did quite a lot of work for Birkdale Council making various vehicles – water carts used to spray the road, cess-pool emptiers, bin carts, wagons etc. – but for some reason the Council were not in the Master Farriers Association – a fact that one day when I started work got me out of a bit of a scrape. One early morning when I was in the smithy on my own, a horse came clamping down the entry and the driver told me that the horse had a shoe loose. The horse was so big that I could nearly walk under his belly. However, I was just considering whether I would even be able to lift his foot, never mind knock nails in, when my father came in and said to me,'Who does this horse belong to?', and when I told him it was the Corporation, he said, 'You must not touch it. They are not in the Shoeing Smiths Association and are not in the Master Farriers Association.' At least it solved my own little dilemma.

In 1904 father did his first car deal. It was a Stanley Steamer with tiller steering. The man who bought it brought along his wife when he came to collect it. Sadly, after leaving the works with the new car and on approaching the first corner, he lost control and crashed into a wall. His wife broke her leg in the accident.

During the next few years I can remember such names as Rover Single Cylinder, Wolseley with a two-cylinder engine mounted crosswise and a three-cylinder Aster Fafnir with built-up crankcase and a left-turning engine. The rear axle actually went on this when it was a lorry. I obtained another axle and fitted it but, alas, when I came to try it out I discovered that I had one forward speed and three reverse, having forgotten that the engine rotated anti-clockwise.

When I was about ten years old, I used to sit on a bracket between the two smithy fires watching the blacksmiths working and I remember one day when my father was away, the lads were talking and larking about and I told my father about this. He usually did not listen to tale telling, usually saying, 'I'll find out if there is anything wrong. Get on with your work.' But in this case he tackled the lads about wasting time so the next time I went into the smithy, two of the lads got hold of me and held me upside down over the water barrel threatening what would happen to me if I told any more tales. Needless to say, I did not.

On another occasion, I went down to the works and saw one of the blacksmith's men bent down down doing something to the horse's foot on his knee. I thought it was one of the lads who had liked a joke. They all wore the same sort of moleskin trousers and the tight backside was too much of a temptation, so I gave it a good kick but what a shock I got. He dropped the horse's foot and turned around. It was the Head Smith and he most certainly did not see the funny side. However, he took it in good part when I, stuttering, told him how sorry I was and explained the mistake and, in fact, he went on to ask me if I would like to accompany him to see the Flying Fairies at the Opera House. He did scene shifting at nights and matinees and he took me up into the flies and sat me in a corner out of the way. It was quite hot as I was near to one of the big limelights, which in those days were worked by acetylene. A boy was working it and changing the colours from time to time, then he would turn a winch which lifted the big water-filled safety steel curtain which had to be lowered and raised twice in every performance to comply with the law.

I could see all that went on on the stage. The chorus girls in those days were more like chorus ladies and they had a precarious time finding work. On the other hard, the fairies were quite young and I would watch with great interest the way the wires were clipped on to concealed belts. Various ropes would be pulled to make the girls appear to fly through the air. It was very cleverly done.

At the end of the pantomime, Charlie asked me if I would like to see his pigs. Apparently, breeding pigs was another way of supplementing his wages. He had the biggest sow I had ever seen or have seen since.

Charlie was a first-class blacksmith and made some wonderful ironwork for the various vehicles. Although he was crabby, he was a very quietly spoken man and only once in later years, when I had started work, did he get cross with me. It was when my father bought a gas engine and placed me in charge. One day when I was polishing the fly wheels, Charlie said to me, 'If you looked after the horse as well as you look after that thing it would make more sense.' Actually, he hated mechanisation, especially the fan that blew the smithy fire. It did 6,000 revolutions a minute and was terribly noisy. Also, a new flux had been invented to facilitate welding the new clincher tyres and Charlie would not use it. I was very sorry when my father insisted and Charlie gave in his notice. However, he started on his own account and we remained friendly and my father would sell him various materials.

One day my father asked me if I would like to go to Liverpool for a load of wood and, of course, I said that I would. My mother thought that at thirteen I was too young to have such responsibility but the people in the next yard to us ran a daily service to Liverpool with their heavy horses and lorries and this had fired my ambition to have a go. The drivers claimed that they walked all the way at the horse's head but I, for one, after about four miles climbed up onto the wagon. I was both tired and frightened and it was still dark and I only had a little candle lamp.

I arrived at the timber yard at about 8 a.m. and was loaded up with various types of wood in the form of long planks and, after roping it on, I set off for Ormskirk, where I arrived just as it was getting dark. A policeman stopped me and asked me what I was doing and how old I was and who had sent me. When I told him it was my father, he said, 'He must have a lot of confidence in you.' I was to leave the lorry to be unloaded at the works the next day and bring home a cart belonging to a Governess that had had a covered top fitted to it.

As if the journey had not been eventful enough for me, just as I was going past the church in Ormskirk, a small crowd of people stopped me and asked if I was going to Southport and, when I said that I was, they asked me if I would take an old lady to her home about two miles away. They told me that it was down a certain lane, which I knew, but what they did not tell me was that she was drunk and when they lifted her in I could see that all her face was bleeding from where she had obviously fallen down. When I arrived at the lane end, I got her out of the cart with some difficulty and I was trying to make her understand that she was home when she fell down in the roadway, just as a heavy cart with two big men in came past and a wheel ran right over her. They got her from under the wheel, but when they saw what had happened to her they had no intention of staying to help me. I was tired and pretty desperate and I had the lamp in my hand. I told them that I would throw the lamp at their heads if they did not give me a hand to lift her into the cart, which eventually they did. I set off at once to take her back to Ormskirk.

Poor old Tommy was very tired and I was reluctantly whipping him to get him to climb the hill up to the church at Ormskirk. I met a policeman and told him what had happened and he gave me directions on how to get to the police station. When I got there and repeated my story they directed me to the hospital when, again, I told my story. They wasted a lot of time trying to find out her name etc. before they put her on a stretcher and took her in.

I got home at about 11 o'clock, after having been on the road for nearly twenty-four hours. My mother was worried stiff at my long absence. The old lady was not dead, but she died the following morning. She had been drinking meths all afternoon, it was revealed at the Inquest. The police had discovered who the who men were and they had to appear at the Inquest. I was not called up to give evidence. The Coroner severely reprimanded the men for not taking any action and for leaving a young boy on his own, especially on a pitch dark night. I have never forgotten that episode, which happened nearly seventy-five years ago. I have always been afraid of the dark ever since then, especially when I was on sentry duty in the middle of the night in the First World War.

When my father bought Tommy, he had been the right-hand horse in a pair drawing a wagonette and on Thursdays he would travel on this road to Ormskirk and he always had a tendency to pull over to the right-hand side and also he would always pull in at the Morris Dancers and the Red Lion. remember some nights we would see shooting stars and the Northern Lights and my father would explain all about them to me.

There was a nasty unlit corner with a deep unguarded ditch alongside, near Heathy Lane on the railway where a little steam carriage called Altcar Bob or Chipped Potato ran. To signal the driver to get on, you had to show a light or strike a match. On more than one occasion our traction engine, which I will be mentioning again later, has pulled cars out of the ditch with its wire rope. My father was once at a committee meeting of the Council regarding an ambulance he was making for them and he brought up the fact that a lamp should be erected at that corner. One of the Councillors, an old farmer, got up and said, 'Nay, people ought to be in bed at that time of neet.' To this day the corner is still not lit up. At the same spot a butcher who had a country round saw a girl running out of the field screaming. He was just about to stop to see what the matter was when a man ran out from the other side and the butcher realised that this had been an attempted hold up. The man galloped off.

In later years we had a little motor lorry and one very foggy night my father had to walk in front with one of the paraffin lamps and he was very careful at this particular corner. Although we had an acetylene head lamp, I still could not see the road as there was no kerb. These lamps wanted a lot of attention. After each use they had to be washed out and cleaned and fresh carbide and water supplied. I was nearly blinded one night when the little rubber bag that equalised pressure backfired and blew up in my face.

When I look back, if we went to Ormskirk, which was about eight miles and back, without any trouble or punctures we thought we had had a marvellous run. One night the engine conked out and although I started it up and it ran for a minute or two, it conked out again. During one of these little runs I happened to go around the back of the vehicle and noticed no exhaust puffing out. When I undid the big nut which fastened the pipe to the silencer the engine roared away. I eventually found that the silencer was full of water.

In later years we had made a small turntable to fasten on to the back of the lorry to which the shafts of the various vehicles were fastened and towed home. It saved so much time that poor old Tommy had to go after eleven faithful years' service. He even went on holiday with us. The family and perhaps friends would go camping in Wales. It would take us about two and a half days but when my father made a motor caravan in 1920, we did the same journey in about two and a half hours. This was on a 1912 Belsize chassis which I had overhauled and fitted heavier T-Ford wheels to the chassis at the rear. There was not even a dipstick in the oil system, but when we were out on a journey, I knew that the engine wanted a bottleful of oil every fifty miles, so I kept a locker full of beer bottles filled with oil.

The clutch was a metal to metal cone and was very fierce. I once tried putting oil on it, then it slipped. This spoke well for the back axle as it was a big strain, especially when starting on an incline. There was also neither electric system nor self-starter and, as the caravan body was very wide, my father made a wooden hand and painted it flesh colour and it swivelled outwards when a handle was turned from inside. If you wanted to go left, your passenger had to drop the window and put his hand out. There was no windscreen wiper but, as the cab was built over the bonnet, the rain had to be very heavy to affect the visibility. The van had an unusual sleeping arrangement and would accommodate six adults. It had an awning which attached to the side and what was termed a 'pigeon locker roof' with opening ventilators and illuminated by a Tilley lamp. It proved to be very reliable, although at odd times everyone but the driver had to get out and push. We had some marvellous holidays and once did 1,000 miles in a week and wherever we went it caused a tremendous amount of interest, being one of the first motor caravans. If we had continued building caravans instead of buses and coaches, we might well have been far better off.

Sometimes in my school holidays from Bury Road School, I would go to Wales to stay at a farm at Berwyn. One time I went to the ticket office and said that I wanted a ticket for 'Glynfrawdy', which I thought was the way it was pronounced but the chap in the booking office said that he had never heard of it, so he asked me how it was spelt. 'Ah,' he said, 'you mean Glynfrdwy.' I would sometimes go and help the farmer there and he would give me various jobs to do. One time I was cutting thistles in one of the fields which ran down to the railway, which was a single track line from Wrexham to Barmouth and I was looking over the fence at the signal box. The signalman came and spoke to me. He was only a young fellow, and he said, 'Would you like to come in and see the box?'.

I hopped over the fence and went up into the signal box and he showed me all the various levers and things. I would help him to clean the lamps and fill them with oil, do any cleaning jobs, boil a kettle on his little coke stove or perhaps even make some toast. The signal box was three quarters of a mile away from a tunnel which was itself three quarters of a mile long and it was quite interesting watching the trains coming out of the tunnel past the signal box. When a train was passing, I had to duck down underneath the windows just in case there were any inspectors on the train as, of course, only the signalman was allowed in the signal box.

This was on a single loop line and the passing point was at this signal box and when the engine came along they had to deposit what they called a staff onto a thing with a sort of cow's horn on it. The fireman had to lean out and put the staff onto this horn and then, further along, grab another one to take them over the next section of line. It was a safety device so that they could not have two trains on the one line at the same time. I was eventually able to work the machine that released this staff. The staff was quite a heavy thing so the signalman would go down the steps and fix it up on the post ready for the next engine to pick it up. Some drivers did not slow down sufficiently and it must have been an awful wrench on the fireman's arm picking it up on the move. Of course, sometimes they would miss it and did not save time because they then had to reverse the engine back to pick it up before they dare go on again.

During this particular holiday quite a few interesting events happened. The first concerned a farmer by the name of Mr Jackson. He used to walk five miles to work in a slate quarry and then he would walk the five miles back again to his farm, where he would have a meal and then get on with his farming. They ploughed one or two fields and had a very old horse called Polly which had not been broken in for ploughing and had to be led. It was my job to lead her along the furrows. One day he went back to the farm for lunch and Mr Jackson had something else to do, so he sent me out to harness old Polly to the plough.

I did this and waited ever so long and when Mr Jackson did not come I thought I would have a go at ploughing myself, so off we set. Unfortunately, the plough was going in the direction of the farm and when we got to the end of the furrow Polly would not stop. The plough went through a dried up patch and sparks went left, right and centre. I dreaded and feared that it would break the thing. However, the farmer came back just in time and stopped Polly. He did not say very much to me about it because he thought I was doing it all in good part.

Another day, I and one of the older lads from the farm were in the field in which there was a nasty bull and this lad got us to throw little stones at the bull's private parts. The bull did not like this, which was quite understandable! He cocked up his tail and gave out a mighty belch and charged after us. I climbed over a fence which must have been about seven or eight feet high, something I could never have done if the bull had not been charging at me.

The next day, the farmer took the same bull to another farm to put it with the cows. On the way back he said to me, 'Now you stand by that lane entrance and, whatever you do, don't let him come past you.'

However, the bull had other ideas and it decided to trot straight towards me. I did not fancy a confrontation like the previous day and stepped to one side. The bull, of course, ran down the lane and the farmer commenced swearing at it in Welsh. We had a mile and a half walk before we found it.

When we got back, our troubles with the unruly creature were not yet over. The farmer put it into the yard and he wanted the bull to go into a certain shed, but, instead, the bull decided to take itself off into one of the stables. The farmer mustered considerable courage and went in after it armed with a pitchfork. It was just like something I had seen in comic cuts as the farmer came tossing out. However, the bull came out and the farmer put him in his own place. I always dreaded another encounter with the beast after those few days.

The nearby railway was a lovely section of line going through the woods and alongside the River Dee. Every night the mail train came along from Barmouth to Birkenhead and it was always pulled by one of the bigger engines. All the carriages would be lit up by gas then, of course, but it was very interesting seeing it come along through the fields down below us. In the daytime most of the engines were Great Western Railway tank engines of the smaller variety but sometimes an express and a big locomotive would come through.

I loved to see the tremendous big cranks with the connecting rods on the outside revolving, and also when they were near to the signal box the driver would shut off the steam and it would give a lovely "chuff chuff". Invariably it was blowing off steam and making a loud noise and after they had picked up the staff they would open the throttle and give a gorgeous snort and steam away.

One beautiful afternoon when we were camping, the farmer caught sight of the local preacher on his bicycle coming to visit us. There were quite a few beer bottles around as we had been having a drink, so everybody set to and gathered up all the bottles in order to hide them. When the minister arrived at the farm, he was asked what he would like to drink and to our amazement he said that he would like a beer if there was any handy!

Among our many escapades on those seemingly long summer holidays was fishing with very crude tackle. Sometimes we were accompanied by other families and all the children would go batheing in the River Dee as it was lovely and clean with a pebble bottom. One gentleman by the name of Mr Snowden, who stayed with us for a time, went fishing and also went into the fields to paint. I remember one particularly fine painting he did of the fields full of corn.

I became friendly with one of the local girls whose father was the Chief Gamekeeper. He was a crabby old blighter. There were four sisters and he always kept a strict eye on them. One day when I was walking through the woods to their house to try and meet this girl a shot rang out and a lot of pellets hit the tree just behind me. Of course I did not see anybody but I thought at the time that it was the old chappie trying to scare me off – which he did. I never went near their house again!

Before the First World War we used to go to Wales with the horse and some vehicle with all the camping equipment etc. Sometimes it was a covered lorry and other times we took a big cart which was called a float. One time when we went with the float my elder brother and I had to take it up to Liverpool to meet with the others who had gone on their bicycles. We had to go through Ormskirk. I was driving and my brother was fast asleep. I decided to take a short cut down this very steep road when, all of a sudden the cart got the better of old Tommy and he could not hold it back. However, he managed to keep on his feet and he swerved sharply round the corner. There were sparks flying from the wheels and then it hit the kerb but, fortunately, it did not do any damage. My brother was thoroughly awake by this time and played hamlet with me for going down that road in the first place. When we travelled through Wales we would take turns riding the bicycles and riding in the cart.

All in all, our annual holidays were quite an adventure. But, inevitably, thoughts did eventually have to turn towards more serious matters – school, apprenticeship . . . and work.

Chapter Three

Schoolday blues and apprenticeship

FOR SOME REASON, I do not remember a great deal about my very early days, in fact, I do not even remember starting school. The only real memory I have is of writing something down associated with the year 1907. Now I do not know really what it was I was writing but the year 1907 was fixed in my mind.

One day I was going to school and I had to pass a grocer's shop on the corner. The grocer always had a big box of eggs which he would take the lid off so that the eggs were on show. There must have been literally thousands - I think they were Chinese eggs.

One lunch time when I was going home for my lunch, I came across a couple of lads fighting. I watched them, walking backwards at the time, and I fell into the box of eggs. I must have broken an awful lot but I did not wait to see how many. I just got up quickly and ran home. Of course, my mother wanted to know why my trousers were in such a mess.

One morning I was in the school playground talking to some of the lads. One boy unfortunately was a little bit on the simple side. Several of the boys were tormenting him about an incident that had happened in a previous grammar lesson. I remember that the boy should have written 'Going, going, gone', but instead he wrote 'Gone, gone, going'. All of a sudden the boy pulled out a penknife and stabbed the boy standing next to me in the stomach - it must have been in the fleshy part because he did not suffer in any way from it. The boy actually lived next door to us, which was only just around the corner from school. I did not know what to do and the boy was pressing his stomach as he ran all the way home. There was never anything said about this at school and it was just hushed up.

I remember being in the school choir, which was called Birkdale Council School Prize Choir. It had won several prizes and our name was on the shield which was competed for by all the schools in Lancashire. From that school I won a scholarship, but I was never all that interested as I was itching to go and work in my father's business. However, six of us went in for this scholarship and five of us won scholarships out of the six that were granted for all of this part of Lancashire. The only boy who did not pass the scholarship was the Assistant Headmaster's son! He would punish his son (who was a bit slow to learn) in front of the whole class and we would all feel terribly sorry for him. However, he made good, as later on in life I met him again and at that time he was a bank manager.

The scholarship was quite a valuable one and it paid all expenses for four years for any school in this part of Lancashire. We had a written scholarship one Saturday morning, I think it was either April or May. I had forgotten all about it but when we were in Wales camping out our letters were forwarded on to us. A letter arrived to say that I had won the scholarship.

My mother and father were delighted but I wasn't. However, when I went back to school my father wanted me to go on to further education. We had a duscussion with the headmaster who told us that there were two schools available, one of which was a 'higher class' school, but from a point of view of learning he recommended the other school. The latter, I did in fact go to, which was called Bootle Technical and the scholarship paid for the fare also. If I remember rightly, all my father had to pay for were my books. I joined in the second year.

Although I was getting restless as I wanted to start work, there were some very interesting interludes at this school. One in particular concerned the woodwork master, who was a Scotsman named Mr Cahoon. He would take us out sometimes into Ince Woods on a kind of nature tour and he would tell us all about the various trees and leaves and numerous other things. One day, he began to tell us about a tree called mahogany and how it originated. He told us that an Irishman had been sitting underneath a tree with one of his pigs and was heard to say, 'My hog and I,' and it is said they called the tree mahogany.

But, of course, that was just a joke. At least I was fairly sure it was!

The school had a good machine shop, with several machines and engines and also a good woodworking shop with quite a lot of facilities. Also the swimming pool was situated next door, which was quite handy and we held some very fine galas there. One could invite one's parents to these and in the interlude the students would entertain. At one of these galas, several students were chasing one another, supposedly trying to catch each other, running round the balcony and then jumping over with all of their clothes on into the deep end of the swimming bath, holding umbrellas pretending they were parachutes. It was very funny.

The girl's school was next door to ours but the playground was out of bounds to us. However, some of the lads would kick the ball over on purpose so that they could go round and pick the ball up. Eventually that was stopped so we would play hockey in the lunchtime instead. It was quite a big playground and the assistant caretaker was a real dab hand at hockey and he would run rings around us. We had ordinary bent sticks which were not very heavy so that we would not hurt ourselves and there were also soft balls with which to play.

Sometimes I would be late for school due to the fact that I had to catch the train at 7.30 a.m. If I was late I would think up some excuse, which more often than not was that it had been foggy on the line. Sometimes it was foggy and it did cause the train to be late. One beautiful clear sunny morning I missed one train and was 20 minutes late, and Mr Crouts, a genial master and a very nice gentleman who was also my geography master – on my arrival in class said, 'Hello Manning, foggy on the line again?"

We played both hockey and football once or twice a week on the games field. One time when I had been playing and had perspired I lay down on the damp grass and this brought on a nasty cold which resulted in double pneumonia and pleurisy. I was very ill indeed and for ten days I was more or less in a coma, I did not eat anything and I remember one night seeing my mother praying at the bottom of my bed. I remember distinctly hearing the doctor say, 'Now he is approaching a crucial time, this will be the turning point. He will either get better or he will die.' It is very odd that I can remember that happening all that time ago. However, my mother carefully nursed me. Of course, there were no antibiotics in those days, it was just a case of hot linseed poultices, Sloan's liniment and various other things to produce heat. It was very painful. There were no district nurses and the neighbours would help one another in times of sickness. I can remember one or two times when a neighbour from across the road came and sat by my bed.

This particular lady had a son, who later went to sea as a midshipman during the First World War. His boat was torpedoed but he was rescued safely.He was a bit of a toughie and told us what a fine time he had had when they had gone ashore in Southern Ireland – all the people had made such a fuss of them. However, he went to sea again on a tramp steamer which was torpedoed and there were only one or two survivors and this particular boy was never found. His mother would not believe that he was dead and when I would come home on leave and go and see her she would have tears in her eyes. Her husband spent several months touring different parts of the world trying to obtain information about any of the ex-crew members who were saved, and any information as to exactly what had happened to his son to enable him to pacify his wife. Sadly they were unable to obtain any information and it was all very sad for me whenever I went to visit her.

When I was well I eventually returned to school again, but my heart was not in it. I told my father that I would like to leave school and start work, but he tried to persuade me to stay on as he wanted me 'to make something of myself'. He would have liked me to have been a bank manager or an accountant or something similar. I did not want this and told my father so. I said, 'Well I just can't get on at school,' and I told him that I could not remember poetry.

I did well in a lot of other subjects and the poetry master was a very nice gentlemen. I remember we were doing *Julius Ceasar* and I was re-capping in the school yard one playtime, when he came up to me and said, 'Now, how is it Manning that you can't remember this material.' So I said, 'Well Sir, it is like this, if I read anything about engineering or mechanics, I can learn it very quickly, but I just cannot seem to memorise this'. After that, he took pity upon me and I never had to write any more lines for not knowing my poetry. When the time came for me to leave the school at Bootle, and I told the headmaster that I was leaving, he called me out in front of the class and asked me what I was going to do. I said that I was going to work with my father and that for the first two years I would be working in the smithy. Of course, there were loud guffaws from several of the lads but I found out in later years that I had made much more progess than some of those so-called rich boys.

There were quite a lot of snobs at the school in Bootle and they looked down on us 'scholarship boys'. I never regretted having only been at the Bootle school for 13 months, although there have been several times when I have thought to myself that I would have been better off if I had stayed for the four years – though, on balance, I don't think so, because my heart was not in it. When my father eventually said that I could join him he said, 'All right, but you will have to start as an apprentice just like all the other lads and you will not receive any benefits. You will just have to rough it like they do.,' I said, 'Fair enough.'

I worked in the old Chatham Road smithy for two years and there was one thing which I did escape, being the boss's son, and that was the traditional 'initiation' which all apprentices had to go through which was terribly embarrassing for a young lad, especially when you had three or four big men holding one lad down and invariably 'debagging' him. Later on in life when I was my own boss I would tell the men that if I caught anybody ill-treating a new apprentice in any way I would sack them immediately because I did not agree with this business of three or four men holding down a little lad.

I started work for my father in the smithy and one of my jobs was that I had to have the smithy fire alight by 7 a.m. in the morning and enough coke crushed to last all day. I found that crushing this coke was as hard as blowing the bellows and using the sledge hammer. After I had been working in the smithy for some time I came upon the idea of making a coke crushing machine run off a gas engine. So, one Saturday afternoon, I went back to the smithy and began to make this contraption which consisted of some upright beams and I found a shaft and some cast iron bearings. It was a bit sloppy but I thought that it would do, so I welded a piece 2 x half an inch about 18 inches long onto this bar. I then drilled one end to accommodate what was to be the shaft which operated the coke crusher.

The connecting rod was a piece of oak and I fastened some metal pieces on the end and started it up, and lo and behold it could crush the coke faster that I could feed it in, so I had to make a big wooden hopper. When my father went to the smithy on the Monday morning, there was a terrific clattering going on. It would make an awful noise and, of course, the piece of metal flying round was very dangerous. However, he said I could continue using it providing I placed a guard around it. This I did and continued to use it for quite a while. But one day a big steel nut got in among the coke and into the coke crusher and, of course, it cracked the cast iron plate and so put it out of action. By this time we were able to buy coke and coal crushed small enough for the smithy fire. The coke crusher was scrapped, but that was my first idea of making something useful and, to my way of thinking, an invention.

This was one of the times in my life when I worked and learned the hard way. I was put to work with one of the senior improvers as a striker and, of course, it was my job to pump the bellows and wield a big hammer all day and turn a big drilling machine which was a two handed job. It had a big fly wheel over the top which revolved at a frightening speed if you turned it very quickly.

I remember one Saturday morning the two other apprentices were drilling the hoops that were going to be used on one of the wheels and when it was lunchtime they wanted to get off early to go to a football match. My father told them they could go when they had finished drilling the hoops but not before. However, they thought to themselves that if they broke the drill then father would have to let them go, so they put an extra bit of pressure on the drill which, of course, broke it. They went to my father and said, 'Sorry boss, broken a drill, we will have to go.' So my father said, 'Oh no you don't, light the smithy fire and I'll sharpen a drill for you.' He took out a drill and resharpened it and he made them go on drilling the holes. In a way they were sorry because they were later than ever getting away. The very same two lads were sent one day to deliver a cab back to Birkdale Station. They were gone for quite a while so father jumped on his bike and went to look for them. They had gone down onto the beach and were playing football. Of course he hauled them back and made them work extra time as punishment.

The head blacksmith was a very strict disciplinarian and if I was found shirking or not doing my job properly, or possibly using bad language, which I had heard the other men use, or various other things, he would give me a good pasting even though I was the boss's son. If I told my father that I had been punished, which would be in the form of a good kick on my backside or a clout across the ear, he would say, 'Well, you must have been doing something wrong, go and get on with you work.'

Having worked in the smithy for some time and having visited several joiners' shops where I had seen a gas engine working the machinery I said to my father, 'Why don't we go in for a gas engine, dad?" He said 'Well I'll think about it.' My father was of the old brigade and was used to doing the job by hand which was always a better job in his estimation. In fact, it proved that later on in years when electric welding came out. I wanted to get an electric welder which was much quicker and more effective than welding in the smithy fire. It was a long time before my father overcame his bias against what he called artificial welding.

When we started making army horse shoes at the beginning of the First World War, various implements were made to facilitate making the shoes and we had a contraption called a jumper which was a very heavy machine with a big capstan wheel on it. It had one fixed bed and one moveable bed so that when you turned the capstan wheel it brought the two beds more or less together.

This jumper machine was a great help. If you got the axle hot and put it in the machine and fixed two clamps to hold it together and then turn the wheel it would squash the material up and so shorten the axle. We had been cutting the material one-and-a-half inches by half an inch. I remember the size was called 10f which meant 10 front (front hooves). We had to cut the lengths off with a sledge hammer and sett which was a long and laborious job.

Father saw us cutting these one day and thinking about the jumper machine he got two pieces of heave 2 inch square cast steel and bolted them onto the jumping machine. We put a bar of wrought iron in and turned the capstan wheel. It sheared the metal off which was very much quicker and easier.

One day my brother and I were working machines near father who was doing some sawing on the bandsaw and my brother started doing a whistle that sounded like a bearing squeaking through shortage of oil. The bearings on the long overhead shafting were oiled by glass bottles filled with oil which were allowed to drip and father, thinking that one was empty, went to look for the step ladders to find out if this was the case. Of course, he found that all the bottles were full and none of the bearings were warm. Needless to say he could not understand what was the matter, until he came down the ladder and saw my brother laughing. He did not think much of the joke – it had interrupted work, but father was a great sport really and took it all in good part eventually. Of course an incident of that nature helped brighten the day.

The lighting at that time was produced by some large gas lamps, each containing three mantles. In the works there were only two poor lights, so father said to me one day, 'Why can't we have electricity, can't we make it?' I told him, 'Oh yes, we can make it because there is no mains cable down our street. So off we went to Liverpool one afternoon to have a look for a dynamo and the only one we found was 50 volts so we asked the people if they could supply us with 50 volt lamp bulbs. We bought the shunt wound dynamo extremely cheap, took it home and I fitted it to the engine and got it working. We then wired the works out. The only problem in having a shunt wound dynamo was that if anybody switched off too many lights the other lights would possibly burn out and, conversely, if there were only a few lights being used the engine would register the firing order by the lamps blinking, increasing in intensity with each firing stroke of the gas engine. Nevertheless, it it was a far better light in the works and we were able to light the whole factory for just sixpence an hour which was the cost involved for running the engine. Eventually, mains cable was supplied to our street and wer were able to motorise because we wanted some extra machinery.

Of course, we did not have to work all the time and there was usually plenty of time for leisure. When we were younger we would go batheing down on the beach at Birkdale, often until the end of October. One evening we went out at dusk and one of the lads who was a good swimmer started to swim out. It was rather rough and he did not know in which direction he was swimming until he saw what he thought was one of the lads smoking a cigarette on the beach. He could see this flashing light and swam to it. It was quite a long way and when ge got there he discovered that in fact it was a flashing buoy which was used to mark one of the channels in the olden days. Of course, when he turned around and looked back, he could then see the lights of the town. After a brief rest and, bearing in mind that the tide was going to be against him, he started to swim back to the beach and fortunately he just made it before exhaustion set in.

On another occasion we were batheing down there on a beautiful day and there was a square tent and we saw a lady and her teenage daughter come out of the water and go into this tent. One or two of the lads eventually lifted up the bottom of the tent and peeped under so I thought that I would also have a look. What a lovely sight it was! But we had to beat a hasty retreat as the mother came out with a bathrobe wrapped around her and threatened what she would do if she caught us and I am quite sure that she would have done all that . . . and more!

Another nice sight was to watch the lifeboat being launched on a practice run. Six huge horses would collect the lifeboat from the lifeboat house and draw it along the beach and into the water. They would be up to their breasts in water, then they would turn it around and the lifeboat men would then launch it. As soon as the boat was afloat, they had to start rowing otherwise the tide coming in would have washed the lifeboat back onto the cart which was a very heavy structure and would surely have damaged the boat. They would row a long way and then come back, sometimes setting the sail up to get to shore. They would then get it onto the launch and trolley again and the horses would come and take it back.

There was a magnificent fleet in Southport of fishing boats ('Nobbies'), all of a standard construction about 30 feel long and each had a little stove. The fishing boats would go out to sea, sometimes for two or three days at a time – in fact until they had a good catch – and then they returned home. It was a splendid sight to see them anchored at the end of the pier, especially if there was a glorious sunset. There would also possibly be other yachts anchored some of which were quite large.

Professor 'Bert' Powsey, as he called himself would dive off an elevated platform at the end of the pier. Sometimes he would ride a bicycle down a plane and fall into the water. There was a rope attached to the bike and his helpers would then haul it back onto the pier again. Powsey made his last dive in 1941, at the age of 75, when he dived into a tank from a portable tower, in Princes Park, Southport. If I remember rightly, the tower was 70 feet high and the tank was only about 12 feet in diameter and just over 3 feet deep. He would dive into this tank from the top of the tower, having made allowances for the wind, of course. Sometimes he would pour inflammable liquid into the tank and set fire to it and then he would dive into the middle of these flames which, of course, would be extinguished as soon as he hit the water. He must have been very adept to dive into a mere three feet of water. I can remember when I have dived off the side of a swimming pool into three feet of water and gone down to the bottom and scraped along it. Professor Powsey would tour the country performing this act.

Another interesting episode was when a French tramp steamer was washed ashore between Ainsdale and Birkdale beach. It was left high and dry and the customs men came to see if there was any contraband on board. They found some bottles of liquor which they simply broke and emptied the contents over the side. The steamer was on the beach for a week or two until they dug a channel around it, strengthened the winch on the deck and attached it to several anchors out at sea. A couple of tugs managed to turn it around so that the bow was facing the sea and then, gradually, when there was a very high tide, they were able to tow it back out to sea again. Luckily there was very little damage sustained but it was quite something to see such a boat high and dry.

Talking about shipping, when I went to Bootle Technical School, we would have a two-hour lunch break and I would hurry my lunch and go down to the docks where there would be all manner of shipping in those days. There was a huge dry dock and the *Mauritania* was in on this particular occasion. It was a magnificent sight to see the four big screws (propellers) and the whole of the hull in dry dock and they gave a good impression of its size.

Around about 1910, my father and two friends helped to form the present Sunday afternoon club Brotherhood Band at Brighton Road Methodist Church. He went to Manchester and bought a lorry load of second hand brass instruments. All the instruments had to be cleaned and needless to say we three lads at home were given the job. I remember holding a small cornet, having begun to clean it, when my elder brother came and took it away from me and gave me a great big double bass instead, which was as tall as me. This double bass took me about three weeks to clean. However, we cleaned all the instruments up nicely. The band was gradually formed and the conductor who, incidentally, was a very good cornet player, travelled to Manchester each day on business. Gradually he got the band together and it turned out to be quite a good one.

At Christmas time they would have street collection, but, due to the fact that there were only gas lamps in the streets at that time, it was very difficult to see the music, so father made some little brackets which the bandsmen fastened to their shoulders with a strap around their waist and a cycle lamp was placed in the bracket. But they had to be very careful not to turn their heads around, otherwise they would get their ear burnt. My elder brother was a cornet player and father played the euphonium and the tenor horn. The band continued for about four years until the outbreak of the First World War. As the bandsmen were gradually being called up, the band was eventually disbanded. As far as I am aware there is only one chappie remaining who was in the band and his name is Bill Jagger. He is a former tram and bus driver and he is now over 90 years of age.

Chapter Four

Trips to a Welsh farm

RELATING back to leisure times and my visits to Wales, we would go into the fields where there was a mountain stream with plenty of water running down. It ran over a waterfall six or eight feet deep and on a very hot day we would go underneath the waterfall and allow water to cascade over us. We did not have any bathing costumes at that time, but we always managed to fashion something out of a handkerchief or the like. There were fish in the stream and we always tried to catch them. There was fresh watercress, too, and although the advice of my doctor's son was not to eat it because of the chance of contamination by the sheep grazing nearby, I never heard of anyone coming to any harm. We didn't eat it.

Sometimes when there would be a train standing in the loop waiting for another train to come by, I used to walk along the other side of the hedge admiring the engine, especially if it was an express. Being somewhat envious of the driver and fireman, who often stood there smoking whilst waiting for the signal to change, I stood and watched until suddenly the fireman decided to put some coal on the fire then that made me beat a hasty retreat. The fireman would always leave coaling the fire until such time as he was through the tunnel because the engine cabs were not enclosed as they are today and consequently they would get absolutely covered in soot in the tunnel. Therefore, they would wait until they arrived at the loop before they put any more coal on the fire.

I recall that the farmer with whom we stayed worked at the local saw mill which belonged to the estate. They would cut selected trees down periodically and saw them up to make gates and for general repairs. The saw was driven by a large waterwheel which was fed from another stream flowing down the mountain. One day the farmer asked us to bring some buckets to the mill in the afternoon. He said that he would turn the water off so that we could collect the fish. We went down with our buckets and he had turned the water off, leaving the poor fish high and dry. We simply had to pick them out and place them in the buckets. Needless to say we had some most enjoyable teas.

Whilst we were larking about one day behind a wall in one of the fields which was adjacent to the main road, a poor old tramp came walking along without a care in the world. What did we do? I do not know who started it, but we picked up a lot of sods which were in a heap and we flung them at the poor chap as he walked past. I have often thought about this and what a dirty trick it had been on our part. Of course, when you are young, you do not look at things in the same light.

Whenever anyone stayed at the farm one of the first things the old farmer would do was to get them to give him a shave. He would sit on the flags outside whilst somebody lathered him and go for the razor – which was never too sharp – and give him a shave. He was a tough old blighter and he would sit there and grin and bear it. One day we were in the kitchen, which was very big and had a flagged floor. The fireplace was recessed and one was able to sit around it in the winter time. One of the girls needed some sugar and the farmer's wife said, 'It's in the cupboard.' It was on the top shelf so she climbed up one or two shelves to reach it when all of a sudden she pulled the cupboard down on top of her. Luckily the door opened and took the full force of the cupboard and fortunately she was unhurt. You should have seen the mess all over the kitchen floor and needless to say the farmer's wife was not at all happy about it.

The farmer's wife would make some delicious bread, great big loaves, and I loved to watch her doing this. She would mix all the dough in a big earthenware bowl and then place the risen dough into tins. She would light a fire about an hour or so before she was ready to bake the bread. When it was ready to go in, they would rake out all the ashes and put the loaves in. I think they placed them on the oven floor and when all the bread was in the oven a wooden door was put on. Then, much to my amazement, she would go down to the cowshed and bring a bucket of cow manure into the bakehouse. Then, using her hands, she would put this manure all around the door to make it heatproof and to hold it in place. I was really astounded by this and quite honestly I did not fancy the bread, but it was so delicious that I overcame my squeamishness.

The butter was also made on the farm and very often I would turn the churn to make the butter, which again was delicious. To enable one to have a good meal at any time all that was needed was some of her bread and butter and some of her boiled eggs, but what a way to seal the furnace door!

Another time when I was staying at the farm the farmer's wife took me with her into Llangollen (which was about four miles away) in a horse and cart. It was a beautiful August day and I managed to see some of the circus before I had to eventually go and meet up with her at the cattle market where she had stabled the horse and cart.

When I was very young, I would help my father when I came home from school and one day I asked him for a job and he said that I could paint a wheel which was standing against the wall. It was quite a heavy wheel and so he have me a brush and some undercoat. It then needed turning around and as my father was busy just a little way away, I decided to turn it around myself. I got hold of it and pulled if off the wall but it started to fall onto me. My father noticed just in time and ran towards me, but slipped and fell down on his back. Luckily, however, he managed to catch the wheel just as it was about to fall on top of me. It would have given me some very nasty injuries indeed. I was subsequently scolded for trying to move the wheel by myself.

My elder brother was a bit of a rebel and one day when a doctor's brougham was in the paint shop having been painted in black and dark coach green and varnished. I do not know what possessed him but he had seen a pot of grey paint and what did he do but get the pot of grey paint and painted over the back of the brougham, all over the beautiful work. Of course it made an awful mess and the painter had to clean it all off. Not surprisingly, my brother was not allowed to go into the paint shop again.

Tommy, our horse, was stabled in the works yard and there was a half door which had a sliding bolt and we would leave the top half open. Somehow, he got to know how to slide the bolt and one Sunday afternoon when there was nobody at work, he slid the bolt and opened the door and went walking up the entry. A lady had left her pantry window open and Tommy must have got a whiff of an apple pie, which he promptly ate! She loved the horse so much that she forgave him.

Another day when he got out it was a working day and he went out into the street looking for some lush green grass, which he found in somebody's garden. When I came out into the yard and saw that the stable door was open I had to go and look for him. I brought him back and had to fix another bolt to the outside of the door, this time lower down which he would try to reach but, of course, could not. He was a dear old horse and we taught him many tricks and when eventually he had to be sold to be replaced by motors, all the family were upset.

I had a little old bike when I was about ten years of age which had a fixed pedal and no brakes. One day my mother sent me into town to get some margarine from the Maypole and returning home down Eastbank Street bridge, absolutely flying along with my feet up on the forks, My tyres got caught in the tram lines and I could not get out of them. I was pulling so hard on the handlebars to get out that they came off in my hand! Promptly followed, of course, by an awful crash. I was all right, but the margarine was squashed.

By the time I had visited Wales several summers, I learned how to operate the train signals during my frequent sojourns at the signal box. I was strong enough at the time to be able to pull the levers to operate most of the signals, with the exception of the distance signal which was three quarters of a mile away, but as it was nearly always set for 'go' I did not often have to ask the signalman to pull this lever for me. I was able to operate a machine that released the staff and about the only thing I could not do was to answer the telephone as invariably it was in Welsh!

It was on one of these idyllic summer's days that I lost part of my childlike innocence. One day when I went down to the box the signalman said 'Oh I am expecting the Inspector coming on the so and so train, so you had better go for a walk for an hour or so,' and he gave me a book to read. I went down through the fields and the meadow. The scenery was beautiful along the River Dee. I found a convenient spot in the sunlight and lay down in the long grass and started to read. I subsequently heard girls' voices and I looked up and saw two girls running down the opposite bank and, to my amazement, they undressed. From what I can remember they went into the water totally unclothed and as the water was fairly shallow they could only lark around and splash about. Eventually they got out and lay in the sun and dried off. Then they just put on their dresses and went away, laughing after having thoroughly enjoyed themselves. I didn't dare get up for I would have severely embarrassed the girls. I had never seen 'big' girls in this way before and when I walked back to the signal box I was rather preoccupied and I am afraid to say that I did not appreciate the lovely wild flowers, wild strawberries and other things which grew in abundance along the railway embankment.

When I was somewhat older I had a driving licence. As I was going home from town one day I saw a motor bike lying in the middle of the road and a lad who was known to me was sitting by the wall. He was very shaken and I asked him what was the matter. He informed me that he had run into the back of a wagon and said, 'I'll never drive that thing again, would you like to buy it? Give me a pound.' I sized up the situation and gave him a pound. I took it back to the works and all that was the matter with it was that the forks had been bent backwards and a tyre punctured. I removed the forks and put them in the smithy fire and straightened them out and refitted them. I mended the puncture. It was a lovely little Royal Enfield twin cylinder, with two speed gears and, of course, very old fashioned handlebars, which were long and straight. You simply pressed one lever one way and it gave you the low gear and if you pressed it the other way it gave you top gear. I went to Wales for the day on the motor bike and on my return journey discovered that I was running short of oil. It was a very hot day and so the engine seized up. I pulled over onto the grass and had a look at the oil level and it was empty. There were no garages for miles, and no railways either, and I had to get home somehow. I set off on my bike again but it would only go for about two miles and then it would seize up again! I would have to wait for it to cool down. The engine in those days had cast iron pistons but it did not do any harm. Of course, in a modern engine the cylinders would have been scored after having run it for a few yards without oil, never mind about forty miles. It took me all day to get home.

My father at this time had another works in Park Road, Ormskirk, and I would go with the little motor lorry and try to teach my father to drive, but he never could get into the swing of it. He would persist in pressing the two pedals, clutch and accelerator, at the same time. There weren't any syncromesh gearboxes then and he would grate the gears terribly, until one day, this persistent mistake led me to get extremely annoyed with him, so I got hold of his leg and pulled it off the pedals and said, 'Don't press both pedals at the same time!' He was a little shocked at this and said, 'Oh it's all right for you, lad, you haven't as much on your mind as I have.'

He never did learn to drive, even though we had vehicles, but in any case there was always one of us to take him out. When my brother joined the services we had to give father lessons on how to ride the little motor bike. We put him in low gear and pushed him off in the direction of Ormskirk, which was about 8 miles away. We told him how to change gear, which was quite simple, and after he had completed his business he returned home. We just happened to be outside our house and heard the motor bike roaring down the road. When he had stopped we noticed that the bike had been in low gear, so we said to him 'Why are you in bottom gear?', and he said, 'Oh well, it went too fast when I pressed it the other way.' We tried to explain to him that by throttling the engine back in top gear it would not go any faster than using the lower gear with the engine revving but apparently he had had an upsetting experience when he was in Ormskirk. The road had been very wet and he had skidded into a policeman and subsequently knocked him down, fortunately unhurt. this incident had upset my father.

I went with my father to Wales for a short holiday and we stayed with a gamekeeper friend of ours by the name of Joe, who lived alone high up on the mountain side. The house was called 'The Bulk' we had many an adventure there. On one occasion he asked me if I would like to go out with him, accompanied by a ferret, to get some rabbits. I agreed and we went up into the mountain and put the ferret in a hole. It subsequently chased out several rabbits which he duly caught and killed. However, the ferret seemed to like it underground and would not come out! Joe had a line attached to the ferret which he tugged gently so that he didn't choke the ferret to death. But still the ferret refused to surface. It just do happened that it was lunchtime and he said to me, 'I'll go and get my lunch now and you can sit and watch the hole and if the ferret comes out grab hold of it and put it in the bag.' I was dreading the ferret coming out, as I did not fancy having to get hold of it. However, I sat there for well over half an hour and it did not appear and when the gamekeeper came back he said, 'We will have to dig him out.' He had brought a shovel with him and eventually we dug him out.

Another day, I had an equally distasteful experience. I had seen a lovely big cowslip root with flowers and I thought that it would be very nice to take home to my mother, so I borrowed a spade and went out to dig it up. Whilst I was digging I came across a snake. I noticed its zig-zag markings which, I later discovered identified the beast as the highly poisonous adder. I did not wait around to study it in any greater depth, however – I was so frightened that I just took to my heels and ran back to the gamekeeper's cottage. When I told him about it he said, 'You should not have run off like that, you should have chopped its tail off. Could you see its tail?' I said, 'Yes.' 'If you chop off a snake's tail it won't or can't sting you,' he informed me.

Being a gamekeeper it quite a precarious occupation and, of course, one of the things that he had to do was to safeguard all the young pheasants, and this is why he was always on the lookout for predators such as crows, magpies, stoats, weasels and such like. One day we came upon a magpie which was caught in a trap that had been set on a sawn-off tree. The gamekeeper went to get hold of it and started pulling it. The magpie was squawking and screeching, needless to say. I asked, 'What are you doing that for?' and he said, 'I am trying to get it down so that I can shoot it.' In fact, outside his cottage he had a string between two trees where he would put all the vermin that he shot so that when his bosses came they would see that he had been doing his job. He would also train dogs for gun use by various gentlemen. He would have them maybe only one or two times and he had to curb his usual quick temper in order to train them properly. It was very interesting watching him.

Dogs sometimes found themselves on the wrong side of Joe, however. There was a canal cutting through one of his fields. He had quite a big acreage to cover and whilst standing on a bridge over the canal one day, a barge came along. The bargees invariably had a whippet dog which they would send out to catch rabbits and various other things for their meals. Joe had seen this bargee put his dog ashore to go rooting for rabbits, so when he got near the bridge, he shouted out to them, 'Call that dog in or I'll shoot it.' The bargee just had to take him at his word and call the whippet in, as Joe most definitely would have shot the dog.

Have you ever thought about smells that stir your imagination and are synonomous with their uses? My earliest memories are of burnt oil and steam; the smell of our traction engine and the Great Western Railway locomotives as they stood at the loopline hissing steam and dirty water. It was a glorious smell. Another olfactory memory is of horses and stables. I can still 'smell' them over seventy years later. Also dairies, railway tracks, the creosote of the sleepers, the smell of brakes being applied on the high pressure trains, burning castor oil and the Isle of Man TT races when watching them race down Bray Hill.

Pigeon lofts had another nice smell - it would get right into your clothes. Fitting shoes on to horses and burning them on to make a good fit was a delightful odour. Dogs would come looking for the piece of hoof that had been trimmed off. Then there was that of heather and bracken and the smell of the swimming baths and the fragrant smell of clean babies. The ozone from the seas and mountain and a host of other smells which as I say you can associate with various things. The only obnoxious smell I ever came across was that of pigstys, which is not a smell that you would like to smell very often!

Experiences come and go but the freshness of youth and of childhood holidays in Wales will remain for ever as a strong and powerful collection of memories. If only one had realised at the time just how dear those memories were to remain and how fresh, even after the passage of more than seventy years!

Chapter Five

The army and the Model-T Ford

I ALWAYS had an ambition to learn how to fly and I told my parents that I was going to try and join up as a pilot in the RFC. My mother did not want me to join up as my elder brother who had been in France for a couple of years would write home about all the horrible sights he had seen. For example, he told us about a pilot who had been shot down and was badly injured. He said that a pilot's life expectancy in France at one period in the First World War was 20 minutes.

This still did not put me off so, unbeknown to my mother, I signed the appropriate papers to join both the RFC and the RNAS. However, a friend told me that if I wanted any excitement I should not join the RNAS, as most of their operations were simply going out at night, flying across to Belgium or Holland and dropping bombs and returning home. Their only form of navigation was by compass, very little navigational information was available at that time and when they eventually did get back they had to be lifted out and put to bed as they were so exhausted after having been in a cramped open cockpit.

I decided to join the RFC. Eventually I had my medical when I was seventeen and a half and I was marked down as A4 which was A1 when I was 18. Being a fit young man I was called up when I reached my eighteenth birthday and received by preliminary training. When the time came for me to be allocated to a regiment I received my papers to report to Grove Park in Kent, which was a MTRASC base. I thought this very strange and when I saw the C.O. I said that I had had the impression that I was to be granted a commission as a fighter pilot. He said, 'Maybe laddie, but we noticed you had engineering experience and we have plenty of pilots but no mechanics.' I felt that I had been conned, especially after having volunteered, but I had to be content. The army made an excuse and sent me for another medical, for although they were short of pilots one had to be perfectly fit.

Meantime, I had been reading all about flying and studying how to fly a plane. I had learned all about the weather and the clouds and many other aspects of flying. I felt sure that I would have got my wings, but the medical board asked if there were any reasons why I should not be marked down as A1 and I told them that I did not know of any. But the final examination was performed by the heart and lung specialist and, although I had declared that I had not had any serious illnesses, I had, in fact, had pleurisy in my younger days. He informed me that I could have another attack whilst in the air which could possibly prove fatal. Therefore, they would not admit me as a pilot.

After this I tried to get into the Inland Water Transport Section of the Royal Engineers, and one of the jobs was to cross the Channel by high speed motor launch and take ammunition across. Apparently I was not quite old enough for that but eventually they placed me in the mechanical transport and I was sent to a company on Salisbury Plain where they marked me down as a driver. I remember going out on a test with several of us in the back of a wagon. Most of them had not driven before and they were making a terrible mess of changing gear. They were crashing the gears and stopping the engine and various other things.

When the names were put up on the order, I was down as a second driver. When I remarked upon this to one of the other fellows, he said, 'Didn't you give the Corporal anything?' and I said, 'What do you mean?' He then said, 'We gave the Corporal five bob for himself.' I had seen him going around the back of the wagon and had wondered what he was up to. Apparently they all bribed him to put their names down as drivers. However, in the end I was posted as a full driver due to the fact they they were so short of drivers and I had a brand new vehicle. It was a tremendously big thing and I was so chuffed with it.

I was busy checking over the tools which one had to sign for, when some chap came up to me and said 'The O.C. wants to see you.' I started to amble on and he called 'On the double or else you'll get into trouble.' So I doubled up and went to this very nice chap who asked me if I had any engineering experience. I told him that I had and he informed me that they were terribly short of mechanics and engineers and that he was going to put me into the workshop. I was very disappointed at this as I would not be able to drive the new vehicle.

However, I soon settled down and one day the Sergeant Major came into the workshop and said, 'You see that pile of snow out there, well underneath there's a wagon with two big ends gone, go and get it put right.' So I said, 'Well where should I put it, Sir?' and he snapped back, 'What do you mean, where should I put it, do you want to put it in my b..... office or something? Just go and get on with it.' I had to go and scoop the snow off this thing and get underneath it, take the sump off and undo the big ends. On that particular engine the piston and connection rod would come out from underneath. This meant that you did not have to lift the cylinder blocks because they were all cast in one piece – it was a very heavy job to lift them on so I was at least spared that. I got the big ends off and took them into the workshop, which was a former bus garage, and I re-metalled them and bore them out, then eventually fitted them back again. You can well imagine what it was like. My hands and fingers were bitterly cold as we did not have any form of heating whatsoever. However, I finished the job and got it going again. From then onwards it was just a matter of working on various vehicles until eventually I gained my two stripes. I was then put in charge of a workshop heavy lorry section.

One day I was going about my work in the garage when the Sergeant Major came up to me and said to me, 'Do you know that you are improperly dressed?' I looked down and I couldn't see what was the matter. He said, 'Have you read the orders this morning?' I replied that I hadn't. 'Well,' he said, 'you know you are supposed to read them every morning, go and read it.' I found out that I had been made a Sergeant, so I went straight away to the Company Officer and asked if it was with pay. Of course, you could be an action NCO without pay; indeed one of the Sergeant Majors was only a Lance Corporal acting Sergeant Major.

I told him that I did not want it if I was going to have the extra responsibility. I did not want a third stripe just to have it stitched on my arm, I wanted paying! So they said that they would see to it that it came through, which it did very shortly. When I was 19 I was put in charge of the whole of the workshop. We had no such thing as stores; we had to make do all the time and we had four blacksmiths amongst other tradesmen. Sometimes we would have to make a gearwheel and if we did not have the correct materials we would have to get the biggest diameter that we had and put it into the smithy fire to get very hot. We would then take it out and get four of the strikers with sledge hammers and batter it until it was spread out to the right diameter.

Of course, this made the metal very hard and it was very difficult to turn them out. We only had primitive tools. There were no such things as tipped tools or high speed steel. It was a very laborious job having to keep sharpening the tools all the time. However, we just had to make do. The adjacent part of the works was used by the light car section. They were very busy and during one of our quieter periods the O.C. asked me to help them out by taking some of their work load.

The first car that came was a Model-T Ford and, of course, I had had a lot of experience of this – I knew them inside out. I could probably have overhauled one blindfolded. There was one particular point with a

Model-T when you wanted to take the transmission bands out. There was a system of epicyclic gears of which there were three sets and the transmission bands would come out of only one spot and, of course, I knew all about this. As we began to strip this Ford down some of the lads were looking over the fence from the car section and were probably thinking to themselves that we were going to make a terrible mess. In fact, we managed it very well indeed, although the engine was very rough.

If I had gone into the RFC I would have been trained on Farman bi-planes which were pushers and being told of a flight instructor who had been telling a student that he had just performed a very rough landing. He pulled a plug from out of his pocket and said to the student, 'Do you see this plug?' and the chap said, 'Yes.' 'Well that was stuck into a chap's kidneys after having made a landing like that, so be a bit more careful in future.

As you are probably aware, most chaps in the army had some form of nickname. They used to call me Graham White after one of the very first aviators. As I have previously said I would stop whatever I was doing and rush outside to see what type of plane was coming overhead. I can remember one day rushing out and there were three Sopwith Camels. I think that they were the first British triplanes to be made. One of the pilots of a Sopwith was called Gustav Hamel. Prior to the war he was a *Daily Mail* fostered pilot, and had flown over all the coasts of Great Britain, and had probably taken note of various locations. One of the planes went missing over the channel, and it was assumed that Gustav Hamel was indeed a German spy, and he had taken the Sopwith to Germany for copying. In August, 1921, he came to astound great crowds at Southport, by flying both very high and very low in his Bleriot, and on an extremely windy day. He had flown all over the country giving demonstrations and flights, gymnastic displays and such like and this particular triplane or bi-plane was lost and never heard of again. At the time it was said that he had gone back to Germany and taken this new Sopwith with him.

The war affected all our lives. Once, my brother Sydney was taking a despatch to the lines when he suddenly came across some Germans in the trenches. He hurriedly turned back but they fired after him. When he got safely back near to our own lines our fellows nearly shot him, as he was coming from the direction of the Germans. He was taken to the officer in charge at the front, who asked him how he came to be in that position and he told him that quite simply he had gone along this particular road. The officer asked him to show him and said that he could not possibly have gone there because there was a sentry on duty. However, my brother was definite that he had been there and that nobody had challenged him. So they went to have a look and when they got there they found that the sentry was dead. He had been shot by a sniper. So my brother had had a very narrow escape indeed. He had several narrow escapes whilst serving in France and in the early days of the war he saw some very nasty sights which the Germans inflicted upon the civilians, especially in Belgium.

At one time I was due to be sent out on a draft to Mesopotamia, and I was very sorry when they took me off it. Later on my mother had three soldiers billeted with her who were also convalescing and they came from Mesopotamia. One of them was a very nice lad indeed. He had some disease or complaint of the stomach through swallowing too much sand. The other two lads were from Burnley. They had short cropped hair and they could eat all that was put before them. The Mesopotamian would sit there and just have milk sops and sadly he gradually wasted away. In the end I felt glad that I had not gone out there – I realised that I could have ended up like him.

I have a number of memories of when I was billeted in Edinburgh. We were billeted in an old barrack room and had to sleep on boards. We had a chap with us who had been in the army for a long time and was a six-bob-a-day man. Anyone who joined the Mechanical Transport as a driver before 1915 was paid six shillings a day to entice them away from civvy street. He had been in the army for quite a long time and this particular night he had been out and had had far too much to drink. He fell down when he was trying to get on a tram and the tram ran over his hand and cut off three of his fingers. He came into our room with the blood dripping all over and he was short of three fingers. We had to dash him off to the hospital straight away and we did not see him again afterwards.

I was on sentry duty one night over an empty camp and my turn was from one to three in the morning. It was quite a long way from the next sentry and we had a certain area to cover marching up and down. At one point I was resting in the sentry box and I heard a scuffling from behind. I was really scared stiff, it was very dark, I had no lights and I wasn't within shouting distance of the next sentry. A big black shape came pounding out but I was relieved to see that it was only a dog.

Another night I was in an air raid when we were billeted in an empty house. We were in the attic and it really was a gorgeous sight from this window. We could see all the search lights around London and the barrages that were being put up. We were, of course, supposed to be in the cellar during an air raid. We had had our orders, but we were enjoying the spectacle so much that we just did not bother to go down into the cellar. Suddenly we heard the Germans coming over – they always made a peculiar sound. We knew it was them and suddenly there was a terrific bang and then another bang and then a thud.

The third sound had been a 500-pound bomb and it had dropped right into the back garden. Fortunately for us it did not explode but if it had it would have blown us all to smithereens. It was very sad indeed to hear all the screams and shouts coming from the surrounding streets. Apparently, an engine had been shunting at the railway station nearby, which had given the Germans a target on which to drop their bombs. The next morning when we looked around we discovered that the station had been destroyed, together with several rows of houses and shops.

When I joined up the girls at the cinema had a collection and they bought for me a silver cigarette case which I still have today. It travelled everywhere with me. We had had some fun at the cinema watching the different films. Sometimes we would have a picnic, especially on a Saturday afternoon. We would all sit on a mat in the hall and the girls would bring sandwiches and we made tea and it was quite a diversion between films as some of the films were in very poor condition. It was quite a small place and the manager would buy cheap films and I remember one particular Saturday night we had sixteen breaks in the films! Sometimes when the film wrapped itself around the sprocket we had to hack it off with a penknife, which took quite a while, so the people in the pit would stamp their feet and as there was no carpet on the floor in the pits it made a tremendous noise as you can well imagine.

At other times the motor generator would break down and we would have to turn the machines by hand. Of course, this took quite a while to change over and sometimes impatient people began to sing, 'Why are we waiting?' Sometimes the film would catch fire if it was going too slow and broke. The arc lamps in those days were so very hot that if you did not shut the gate quickly the film would catch fire and although it had fire traps underneath the top spool, they were never very efficient.

If we had a fire we had to quickly cut the film and let it go on the concrete floor and then stamp it out. We also had wet blankets hanging up and buckets full of sand. It could be a pretty hazardous occupation sometimes, but it was quite a rewarding job and full of interest.

Later on, after I had been demobbed from the army, I returned to the cinema and became very friendly with the manager. He had a GN car which was called a cycle car. It had wire spoked wheels and quite a big air-cooled twin engine. It was all chain driven and one night we went out to Blackpool. On the way back we ran into a bank of fog. The car left the road and crashed into a fence. Happily, he had managed to dodge between two concrete posts and hit the wire and bounced off again.

On another occasion, the three of us wanted to go to visit the power station on the railway at Aintree where another one of our friends was an engineer. There was only room for two in this car but it had a very flat body. We had to take turns sitting on the back and clinging on for grim death to the hood. The driver thought it was a huge joke trying to shake us off and as the car had no differential it would hop round the corners, so you had to be very careful not to fall off and hold on tightly.

It was very interesting visiting the power station as we were able to see all the batteries being used as standbys for the railway supply. Each one was 660 volts and each accumulator was about three feet tall. The engineer warned us when we were walking around to keep our hands to our sides as the high voltage had a tendency to attract one and in a particular place there was a mark on the floor where someone had electrocuted himself by touching one of the cells.

Whilst we were there, there was a terrific explosion. Apparently it was one of the breakers coming out and some driver had been studding up too quickly on a train and the breaker had blown. They had to wait for a minute or two before putting the breaker back in again in case anybody was hung up on the mains anywhere and it was quite interesting to watch them change from one generator to another, synchronise the speed before they changed over from one dynamo to another.

Those days before and during the war hold a vast number of memories. Of course, motor cars were becoming far more common and many of the things which I recall from that period centre around these new-fangled horseless carriages. Just before the First World War, my father bought a car from a gentleman at the fairground. This gentleman owned the captive 'Flying Machine' (invented by Sir Hiram Maxim, of machine gun fame) – established about 1906, taken down c.1934. It was quite a big affair with a central mast and other masts and cables projecting outwards. It was revolved by a big gas traction engine and the faster it went the further the boats swung out. If you were sitting on the inside you would be looking up at the sky in next to no time and if you were on the other side you could see the people down below. Sometimes, of course, it made you quite dizzy and I have often thought since how strong it must have been as the centrifugal force must have been quite strong when they were at top speed. Some of the attendants would be dressed as sailors and would stand in the cables which suspended the boats and would hang there, just as an advert I suppose.

We did not have any facilities for towing so in order to collect the car from the man at the fairground father told my brother and me to take Tommy, our horse, down to the fairground and bring back the car. We went and harnessed Tommy to the front of the car and my brother was leading. The road was quite steep as we left the fairground and I was steering. It was quite a small steering wheel and it was pretty hard work. We had, however, about two miles to go to get back to the works. We kept coming across people we knew and once or twice they gave us a cheer. Eventually my brother said to me 'Here take the reins, you will have to drive him,' and he walked along the pavement. He would not be seen leading the horse so I had quite a job driving the horse and steering the car, being careful not to let it run into his heels, as we only had a very short trace on. In fact the other week I was telling my doctor, who is a rally driver, that I was possibly one of the very few people to have driven both a car and a horse at the same time.

The car was one of those little old open tourers, two-seater, and I think it was called either a Star or an Astra, which had come by rail from somewhere. Apparently, the porter, who had unloaded the car pushed it and it came down on an incline and he grabbed what he thought was the brake but was, in fact, the gear lever and it stripped some of the gears in the gearbox, so we had to have new gear wheels made. Of course, in those days the gear wheels were not made out of good quality steel and very often they would shed teeth just by virtue of changing gear very roughly. If you did not do what we called double declutching there would be a horrible scraping and scratching of gears.

Few cars, however, held a more important and affectionate place in my memory than the Model-T. The Model-T Ford was called the flying bedstead, principally because of the very light chassis which was only one eighth steel and about two inches by one inch, though, despite this I must admit I never remember seeing a bent one. Also, the drive shafts were of a relatively thin material, but there again, I never saw one twisted off. Of course, the metal and steel companies in America were amongst the finest makers of metal in the world, besides Krupps in Germany, but they certainly knew how to make their alloys.

In 1921, after my father had made a motor caravan, he entered it into the Preston Guild Procession and it was on a boiling hot Saturday. We had several miles to go in the procession and we had to stop at one point as the pedals were so hot they were burning my feet. When we stopped there was a howl from the spectators on the pavement as they could not see what was going on. Father jumped out quickly with a can of water and as he undid the radiator cap clouds of steam came out. We could not wait for it to cool down so we had to just fill it up and off we went again. Today, if one put cold water straight into an engine you would possibly end up with a cracked cylinder.

If you forgot to retard the ignition, which you had to do on starting them, as there were no self starters on the early models, the engine would kick back. You had to be very wary because when they did kick back very often the handle would catch your shin with a mighty crack. They did not have any spare wheels on the early models. They had what was called a Stepney wheel which was just a tyre and rim which you clipped onto the wheel to get you home. If it was on the front wheel itmade it very difficult to steer as you had two tyres on one side at the front.

Although it was all very roughly made and cast, the exhaust system would last far longer than they do today. You could go for a long, long time on one silencer and exhaust pipe. Starting from cold was quite a procedure, though; the clutches were multiplate, and when the oil was thick the plates did not separate very easily.

The Ford handbrake was a very modest affair, meant purely to hold you when parking, so very often in the cold weather you had to jack one wheel up to start the engine which made it easier to turn over, but if you forgot to scotch the wheel, it became a hazard as the Ford jack was a very flimsy affair and if you opened the throttle too wide and the engine went off with a roar it would bounce about on the jack. Also, if you did not scotch the wheel and it happened to start without being jacked up, the thing would creep forward.

One of our customers, who was a farmer, had been warned about this happening when I taught him to drive. However, he failed to do this one morning and he started up in the garage and it crushed him against the wall and he sustained injuries from which he later died. Driving was not what you would call pleasant by modern-day standards. When eventually the self starters were brought out, together with a different system of producing electricity by modern magneto or coil, it made it far easier. They also eventually started issuing spare wheels and when this happened, a firm in Birmingham made several Model-T Ford parts which you were able to buy far cheaper than buying direct from Ford and they issued kits for altering the existing wheels. I enjoyed this job of taking the wheels off and cutting off the rivets which held them onto the hub plates and fitting the new hubs with studs on and making it possible to have a spare wheel. This company also made a radiator which was far more efficient than the standard Ford radiator which was a very cheap affair. These were made from brass and looked quite good and you were able to travel much further without having to replenish the water in your radiator if you had one fitted.

One time, later on when we were selling Ford cars, we had a job to get a delivery and I came to count up the cost, from the catalogue, the total cost of buying all the spare parts came to about ten times as much as the cost of a chassis. Needless to say that idea had to be ruled out.

Soon after the First World War there was a British firm which brought out an extension called a Bako which made the Ford into a

30cwt capacity vehicle by taking off the Ford rear wheels and fitting a sprocket and mounting the chassis which was supplied. The chassis frame had a solid back axle and, of course, solid tyres on the wooden wheels. It was quite a presentable commercial chassis.

An American firm called the Smiths Formatruck, supplied one of these extensions and it made a far better and stronger job than the Bako and we sold quite a lot of them. I also enjoyed getting second-hand touring cars for farmers, and taking the body off and fitting this Smiths Formatruck which also was quite a strong three by one and a half channel extension, which went right from the front end of the Ford chassis and extended well out of the rear and there again a sprocket was fitted onto the Ford T axle and chain driven to much stronger wheels than the ones on the Bako.

Father made one of the very first horse boxes in 1921 on one of these and it proved very popular with the farmers and also food distributors. I remember we sold four to one particular farm, and the caravan to which I have previously referred to went down to London to the Motor Show.

We set off for London with my father, a friend and his wife and we were well down the country on the first day when we had a puncture in the front wheel. (The rear wheels were solid tyres.) I pulled in and father had to walk about three miles in order to have the puncture repaired. We took the inner tube out and he walked to the garage. He came back and refitted it and we drove a few more miles and then we pulled off the roadway. We intended sleeping in it as it slept six and was quite spacious. Father went to a farm, I can't remember why, but he went down the lane to the farm. I don't know if it was to get water or milk but when he came back he was quite tipsy – they had been giving him apple cider drink!

The next day we set off towards London and came across a very long hill on the other side of Oxford and I kept the vehicle in check really because on the Model-T Ford you could use the reverse pedal as a brake, providing you did not press the other pedal which was the high and low gear. I was alternately pressing the reverse pedal and the brake pedal going down this hill and I also had the big brake on. Eventually, the transmission bands burned out on both the reverse and the brake pedal and the caravan set off at a rare old pace down the hill, which was long and straight. I could see well down it but to gain extra pull on this brake lever I was steering with my knees and pulling with all my might with both hands on the brake lever to help retard the speed. If there had been anything in the way there would have been a mighty crash because it was just out of control. We then had to pull in and I had to take out the transmission bands, (in those days you always took as many tools with you as you could) and then take them to a Ford agent, have them replaced with new ones taken them back and refit them.

We duly arrived in London but did not actually go into the Motor Show. We remained outside as we had no stand inside but it was amazing the amount of attention that the caravan received as it was one of the very first.

Father also made what we termed cattle trucks, although they were used to carry horses, cows, sheep, pigs and other animals. He had the idea of making a dual purpose body for cattle dealers or farmers, by adding side pieces whdich we made onto the lorry flaps.

As a lot of my writing is about improvements, I thought windscreens would be an interesting subject. I don't remember any of our veterans having windscreens. In fact the first that I recall was the Model-T Ford that had a very tall two-piece screen, the top half hanging from the centre and down the inside. This, of course, let in the rain and cold winds. Sometimes when my mother was in the back seat, she would put her umbrella up instead of pulling the hood over, and it was not as draughty. When we started building cabs for lorries or vans, we made our own screens, but hung them from the top and outwards, so keeping a lot of rain out when opened.

Some of our army vehicles had screens, none had hoods that could be pulled over, and a piece of tarpaulin could be unrolled and pulled up under one's chin, but of course all down round your legs was open to the elements, as indeed our first cabs were. Eventually half doors were fitted, and as I look back, it was quite a while before enclosed cabs were made with full depth doors, and of course hand-operated wipers. Now they even fit bunks, facilities for cooking and heated cabs, especially on long-distance vehicles.

Although safety glass had been on the English market since before the war, it was not until 1927 that it became increasingly in demand for the cheaper sort of car. The reason it took so long to reach this stage may have something to do with the low traffic density of the early years, which kept the risk of accidents down to a reasonable level. On the other hand, it may have been that the average motorist had even less imagination than he has now. Since 1962 Triplex have been making glass, five factories now make five million square metres a year for road vehicles, also a new Aircraft and Special Products Division makes windscreens for other forms of transport. Triplex is a subsidiary of Pilkington Bros. Ltd. and inventor of the float glass process, which has been licensed to all the world's leading glass manufacturers. I must thank Pilkington Glass Co. Ltd. for enabling us access to their considerable archives. It is most interesting reading about all the set-backs and experimentation overcoming difficulties over so many years.

It amazes me how they can make these wrap-around screens with so much precision in safety and in keeping out the weather. The general public have to thank Pilkingtons' for providing so much of our daily comfort in keeping us warm and dry in our homes, on land, sea and air travelling. I hope that next time you are out in your car in a howling gale you are snug and comfortable, and that you think of those people including myself who used to be thoroughly miserable very often, before windscreens were heated, tightly fitted and condensation-free. Windscreens were made possible mainly by Pilkingtons.

My mother and father helped to form both a brotherhood and a sisterhood in the earlier part of the century and my brothers and I attended, then my sons. A fourth generation was attending when our local chapel was demolished. The organ was to be sold, I think it was for about £500, but unfortunately vandals got into the church and drove a pole through the glass doors of the organ and damaged several of the pipes, so it was of no real value to anyone thinking of buying it.

When I was thinking about making a model fairground organ I was able to obtain several of the smaller pipes and parts of the bellows which were made of bone dry pine to make other parts of the church organ. The same organ is now making a lot of money for the Cancer Research Fund, so parts of the old organ were put to good use.

I also asked permission to use the banner which had preceeded the church band when they were out marching. Having obtained permission I returned only to find that the same vandals who had broken in had also had a bonfire and destroyed several things, including the banner, hymn books and bibles. It was very sad.

My father in his younger days rode a penny farthing bike. He also did a lot of skating in winter on the Norfolk Broads, where you were able to skate for miles and miles at very high speeds. Eventually, when he came to Southport, he bought himself a bike with a two-speed gear which was indeed a luxury. Sometimes he would set off at weekends and take his friend Mr Brerton with him. He was a councillor and a JP and lived opposite to us.

I sometimes think about the old times and wonder whether they really were good times. For example, when my grandmother was very ill and bedridden she lived in a little back bedroom. She was unable to read in the evenings as the only form of lighting was by candlelight. There were, of course, no radios at that time and it followed that there was very little for a bedridden person to do, so consequently she would ask me to read to her from the Bible.

There was a grate in this room but it was too close to the bed so she was unable to have a fire. There were, of course, no electric fires in those days. I remember also when I was very young seeing my mother in bed. I was unaware of what was the matter with her and I can remember seeing horrible leeches crawling on her.

I do not remember there being any district nurses available although neighbours and friends would nurse one another in times of sickness. There were not many forms of pain killers available and one just had to suffer. When anyone was sick loads of sand was distributed on the road for some distance each way outside to lessen the noise caused by vehicles and left for a few days until the patient either died or recovered. Nowadays, of course, we are able to take a pill to do the same job and to remove the pain.

There were no such luxuries as gas stoves or washing machines. My mother's hands used to be red raw with religiously washing each Monday morning using strong soda, as there was very little in the way of soap.

We had to make our own enjoyment and pleasure and we did this by having musical evenings, whist drives and sometimes we would have spiritual meetings. Of course, we always attended events at the church.

We also had lantern lectures which were prior to the cinema days, perhaps slides about a country, missionaries or other interesting items, but the fact still remains that generally there appeared to be a greater degree of friendliness amongst neighbours which sadly we do not seem to see these days. There is so much envy and selfishness.

There was a time when we thought that our youngest son would join the ministry as he always did well in his religious examinations but sadly it was not meant to be. My eldest sone at one time wanted to be a medical missionary but his wife had a collapsed lung and the medical authorities would not pass her fit to travel abroad. He had to be content practising medicine in this country. However, he has done very well for himself and is now a Fellow of the Royal College of Occupational Medicine. He lectures up and down the country and has also lectured in America and Norway.

I also had a lovely little sister who died of meningitis when she was two years of age, but nowadays one has every chance of recovering from this disease.

I have seen so much progress made in my time, but I often think when I hear people complaining now about the lack of facilities if they only knew what one had to do in the olden days. I do think their outlook would possibly be very different.

About the same time we had taken a White Steam car in part exchange for a new van which we had made and as the age of steam cars had passed owing to the reliability, cleanliness and general improvements of petrol driven cars, we had to scrap the White Steam car. I remember getting a sledge hammer to it and knocking it all to pieces. It had a beautiful engine which was a three-cylinder double-acting version and it really was a shame to break it up. We also had a very reliable little car called an Aster which was a three cylinder model. If only we had any of these vehicles now they would be worth a fortune.

Before I joined the army I wanted to make my mother more comfortable at home. We always wanted her to move to a bigger house but she would never leave this particular house where we lived for many years. In the very early days it did not have a water closset; it had what was called an ashpit. Everything went into this ashpit and each morning we were supposed to sprinkle ashes inside and the Corporation supplied chloride lime to sprinkle over it each day. Periodically men from the Corporation would come and empty it. It was a rare treat when we turned over to what at that time was a modern water closet which, of course, was outside in the yard and this meant having to go out in all weathers across the yard to the toilet.

I wanted to cover the yard in and make a conservatory for my mother. This I did in my off duty moments, so to speak. I completed the framework which was quite big. My father had been a keen photographer and he had a lot of half plate glass negatives which I intended to use as windows. I dipped these in hot water in order to clean them. I had previously asked father if I could buy some glass for the conservatory, but he didn't know why I wanted to build a place like that. However, when he saw the framework up and saw me trying to clean all these glass plates he said, 'Go and order some proper safety glass and let's do the job properly'. I think by this time he could see the benefit of being able to go across the yard to the toilet in comfort because it was completely covered in at the sides. We also had a wash house in the yard (which you could now get to under cover) which I later made into a nice bathroom. Well I am saying nice, actually we had to light the boiler fire whenever we wanted to have a bath, but it was such a nice warm place.

I had this idea of making my mother a kind of bungalow continuing from the conservatory right across the garden. We had bought some chassis from Italy and they came in huge wooden packing cases and I made the wooden floor and everything else out of these. I then purchased an ex-army coke stove and fitted it into the wash house chimney and the whole family would spend most of their time in this bungalow instead of in the house, as it was so nice being able to look out into the garden. I had made all kinds of archways and my mother had planted roses. It was very nice and comfortable and warm looking out into such a lovely garden. Every Saturday evening my father invited someone from the local chip shop and they would play cards, so all my work was put to good use.

The house was only lit by gas, but this was another great improvement from using candles before gas was introduced. Originally there were the ordinary gas jets which gave a very poor light and then a German firm invented the mantle which gave an incandescent light which was a great improvement. Then came the advent of electricity, but we did not have a cable down our road at the time so I bought a single cylinder car engine with automatic inlet valve which was ideal for converting into gas and I cast a shaped base for it and cast some holding down bolts in the concrete and bolted it all down and fitted this engine up in the yard, still under cover, of course. I bought a 12-volt dynamo which I used by a chain from the engine and once I got it going it proved to be quite reliable. When it was generating, every explosion was quite a thud and in the end it annoyed mother. I think she was more nervous of it than anything else as I had strung wire about the house and on the pantry floor there was a system of batteries, the old leclarche batteries which one had to fill up with liquid. It was quite a good storage system but, of course, really smelly and dirty with all the liquid and sometimes it would froth over. In the end my mother got so nervous that I had to scrap this system and take it all out. It had given us quite a good service for a while.

Chapter Six

Soldiering On

BEFORE I gained my stripes, I quite often helped in the testing of army vehicles. On one occasion, there were two wagons ready for testing, so the Sergeant, who was the tester, came for me. He wasn't a mechanic and actually he knew very little about vehicles. He had got this post by being a bit of a favourite. I remember the very first wagon which he tested. He did not know how to operate the accelerator! You always had to anchor your heel and swivel it side to side and he did not know about this so he sent for me and asked me how to work it. I can remember thinking to myself, 'Well, he's going to be a good chap to test the vehicle if he doesn't even know how to drive it'.

However, we went out into the country and we came down a very narrow road. He was in the front and he passed some other vehicles with very little room to spare. When I came to pass one particular vehicle it had swerved a little and this meant that I had to pull on to the grass verge and as soon as my front wheel hit the grass, of course, it wrenched the steering out of my hand and shot me into the ditch and the lorry was almost on its side in the ditch. Of course, the Sergeant said that there was plenty of room, but I knew there wasn't. We managed to get the chains off the back somehow and got some bolts and fastened them together and anchored them on chains. We did a bit of digging and borrowed planks of wood from a farmer and eventually managed to get it right back on the road again.

I remember one particular occasion, when I was testing a wagon, I was going over a railway bridge which had a latticework side and the left hand wheel seized up. In those days there were no ball or roller bearings – they were plain brass bushes. They had forgotten to put a split pin in the nut and it was left-hand thread, so when this wheel got hot and expanded, it turned the nut dead tight and wrenched the steering from out of my hand, but luckily it did not do a lot of damage.

The very next day I was reversing a wagon out of the garage. There was very little room and I had to keep looking around me in order to get past several obstacles. All of a sudden someone shouted and when I looked down I had trapped a man. Fortunately I had not hurt him as he had shouted just in time. I was only going very slowly but when I saw the Staff Sergeant coming towards me I thought to myself, 'Oh dear, I'm going to catch it now'. However, he played hamlet with this chap for not getting out of the way and for standing there waiting until I crushed him instead of shouting for me to stop.

One of the first jobs I was given when I was stationed at a camp outside Wilton was to overhaul some brakes on a big wagon called a haley. After I had lined the brakes I told the Workshop Sergeant. He said, 'Well hang on I will get the Sergeant Tester to come and take it out and test it'. We took the wagon down some really beautiful lanes and then we went bac to the workshop in order for the Sergeant Tester to make his report.

The Sergeant Major came into the workshop. He was a little fat man, who had served in South Africa and was a Jew. He asked me, 'How did she go?' and I stuck my chest out and said, 'Oh very well indeed'. 'How the bloody hell do you know?' he shouted. Of course, I was only young and I could have cried when he spoke to me in this manner but I often thought about this episode later on and I would think to myself if he had been sent over to France he wouldn't last very long because somebody was sure to pop him off.

We had a Corporal who had been a Cambridge undergraduate and one day he was talking to the same Sergeant Major with his hands in his pockets. I was amazed when I saw this as you were supposed to stand to attention when you were addressing a warrant officer. Nevertheless, he stood with his hands in his pockets and the Sergeant Major told him to take his hands out of his pockets. However, he wouldn't, it subsequently turned out that the Corporal had studied the King's Army Rules and Regulations. Apparently it was a big thick book and he had become acquainted with most of the rules and needless to say he knew just how far to go. I would never dare do anything like that.

The mess hut was right at the top of the line of huts and we used to have to go for breakfast and we had to take a plate with us. We would stand in a queue and then some porridge would be dumped on the plate together with a piece of fatty bacon. Of course, you had to have them both on the same plate because by the time you got back to your hut, especially if you were in one of the far huts, the food would be cold. We had no canteen as such, but there was an elderly gentleman who ran a shop. He was an old skinflint and he would take as much money as he could from us.

We had to make our own entertainment and the Mechanical

Sergeant Major, who had been in the retreat from Mons, would arrange concerts and he would join in.

He had quite a nice voice and he used to sing love songs. He had heard me singing one time whilst I was working on a lorry, 'I've got a motto – always merry and bright'. He put me down on the programme as 'The Baby Sergeant'.

When I saw this, I went to him and said, 'I can't sing'. 'Oh yes you can, I have heard you', he declared.

When the actual night of the concert arrived I was very reluctant to go on the stage, but some of the lads carried me on and I had to sing. Of course, they all joined in with the chorus and from then onwards I had to sing this song at all our concerts.

One Boxing Day, a Sergeant friend of mine and myself decided to walk to the ruins of Sarem. It was a beautiful dry frosty day. The ruins were made of flintstone, which was very unusual. Altogether we had walked 28 miles by the time we arrived back in the evening.

One day three of us were out in the country testing a vehicle which had an AEC switch on the dash and you had to reach forward with your foot, (it was spring loaded and could be switched off). What we used to do was to start off and then switch it off and on again quickly. Of course, there were big silencers on these vehicles and the silencer would get full of gas and, very often, as soon as you let the switch go there was a terrific explosion. I used to set mine like this and then listen and I could hear the other lads in the distance signalling to each other. However, one day the silencers burst as a result of the explosion and, of course, the Sergeant Major sent for me. I suppose he realised that boys will be boys but nevertheless he gave me a good dressing down as the silencer had to be replaced with a new one.

Once, I was Corporal of the Guard and we had to sleep in a hut at the top of the car park. Early one morning one of the NCOs came and played a trick on me. He came in with this other Corporal and got hold of all my blankets in a bundle, carried me outside and deposited me on the tarmac, which he thought was a huge joke. I did not think it was very funny having to get up with my long johns on and get hold of my blankets and come back into the hut and get dressed again.

Army life lacked many creature comforts, of course. We had no beds or anything like that, just three boards on two little tressles and a straw mattress. We had no canteen or YMCA and in the huts at night we had to make our own enjoyment. Of course the lads would play cards for small amounts of money and sometimes they would start fighting, perhaps over a halfpenny. I had a box of paints which I had first bought when I joined the army and I used to paint autograph books etc. by candlelight.

As a result of the extreme cold, instead of sleeping on the three boards and the short tressles, we would prop two boards up alongside so that it made a sort of bunk and we would sleep on the floor just on the palliasse. The place was full of rats and sometimes in the night you could hear them scuttling about in the rafters. Occasionally, one would drop off the rafters and sometimes onto your bed. One Christmas time one of the rats could be seen dragging off a whole turkey which the Sergeants were going to have for Christmas. The turkey was dragged out of sight under the hut and was never recovered. They really were filthy things.

I was sent out at a later date to do some alterations to the car park. We had a new fleet of AEC wagons, 45 in all, with 114.45 hp Tyler engines. They had a half compression device on them which consisted of pulling out a lever which pulled the camshaft along to a different set of camms which had a very small lift which let some of the compression out so that you would be able to turn the engine far more easily. After they had been on the road for a few weeks the wagons were coming in with broken valve springs so the OC sent me to find out why and I discovered that the camshaft was spring loaded end-wise and apparently the spring wasn't strong enough and the camshaft was revolving to and fro. The camshaft was changing and causing the valve to open at the wrong time and the valve springs were breaking. The OC asked me what I recommended should be done, so I informed him that as far as I could see the only thing was to fix the lever so that they couldn't use the half compression device. He thought that this was a very good idea so I made a lot of these levers and went around all the various depots taking off the existing spring levers and fitting the new levers on, which had a couple of nuts behind a bracket which held the camshaft. After that we didn't have any trouble with them. But I got into trouble with the drivers. 'How the hell do you expect us to start them on full compression?' However, the OC said that they would just have to find ways and means of doing so as we could not have continued having all the damages repaired.

I had one of the very first Triumph motor bikes and side car to have a gearbox, which was called a chain come belt. It had a chain to the gearbox and then a belt to the rear wheel. Before this the rear wheel was a Sturmy Archer three speed, but it would give quite a lot of trouble. When I was coming out of the car park one day having not ridden one of these Triumphs before, it wasn't firing very regularly and the Adjutant was standing talking to somebody and as I went past he shouted to me 'Give it some air.' There were two levers, one for gas and one for air. I immediately opened the air control and it chipped on and fired every stroke and it never gave a bit of trouble after that.

We had a load of new Commer three-ton lorries delivered one day and they were very well made. The king pins and the front axle had ballbearings which were a completely new innovation and the only faults were that they were chain driven, but they had very efficient covers over the chains. The universal joints were simply a three-legged star, as it were, with big rubber buffers on. There was no direct connection between the two drives and it was perfectly quiet and never needed any attention or any greasing and I could never understand why this system did not cotton on, but it didn't.

They had pre-selector gearboxes and when I once had to take a convoy of 30 or so, none of the drivers had driven this particular vehicle before, so we had to use the clutch to start off and put it into first gear and open the throttle. There wasn't an accelerator; the throttle came up through the centre of the steering column and you had to pull this lever down to rev your engine up until you would put it into the next gear and then close the throttle quickly and you could hear it jump into gear and then just open the throttle again gradually and do the same with the top gear. There were three speeds, but it was awful for me hearing the crashing of the gears as they were all doing the wrong thing. In fact there was one driver, an older man, who was very nervous and in the end I had to put my motorbike in the back of this vehicle and drive it the rest of the journey.

When the war ended, I did not get demobbed immediately. In fact I was put on a disposal board as I had all the records of most of the vehicles. We had to move our depot lock, stock and barrel as the bus garage we had been using was needed by the bus company once again after the war. We had to move all the equipment, but we did not have any fork-lift trucks or cranes or anything like that. We had one or two big machines and I got them into my FWD wagon and we then set off. We had about 50 miles to go to a place called Hitchin. We came to a hill which was so steep that my engine just would not pull my load. I had about 7 tons on and one of the chaps hopped out and put a stone under the back wheel and I tried one of our other lorries in front to give us a tow but our combined efforts just could not move this heavy load. There just happened to be a steam roller preparing the road so I asked him to come and hitch on to our tow rope and he moved us up the hill.

When eventually we arrived at the depot we had to unload just with crowbars, levers and different things. As we were getting one big load off using heels and levers, I said to one of the lads, 'Don't put your fingers on top of any of the wood, grip hold of it by the side.' However, we progressed and soon there was a terrific shout and when I looked this lad's thumb was stuck on the top of one of the heels, the thing had slipped and sliced his thumb right off. He was a tough little lad from

Oldham and he was laughing about it, but that same night he was in very severe pain having lost his thumb.

Whilst we were unloading the lorry, the Sergeant Major came and told us that he wanted us to unload before lunch. We had managed to get most of the stuff out and then I said to one of the seven lads that were with me, 'Come on the Sergeant Major wants us to unload this before we have our dinner.' There was a lot of moaning and groaning and they said, 'Oh well, we want our dinner.' They went and left me and I could have put them on a peg and got them into very serious trouble. However, one lad came back and we set to jack up this machine and put rollers underneath it and I could see these other lads in the dining room looking out through the window. Eventually they came back one after the other and helped me to get unloaded and when we had finished I said, 'Right lads, you can have the rest of the afternoon off now.' Well as I say I could have put them on the peg and they could possibly have been court martialed through not obeying an NCO.

I became friendly with one of the girls at our headquarters. After the war had ended we had civilians working for us as the lads just kept on being demobbed and were replaced by civilians. In some cases they could do what the army lads had been doing and I became very friendly with this girl who had been in the stores and she invited me to her home. She lived in a village about 5 miles outside the town. I went on my motor bike for the day to see some wagons and when I returned and went into the mess at night, one of the Sergeants, who was a tremendously fat little guy, a Londoner, said, 'Oh, we had a treat today, we were kidding your girlfriend and we turned her upside down amongst other things'. I was annoyed even more when I tackled her about it as she seemed to have enjoyed it.

In fact we became engaged and were intending eventually to be married. We had even decided on a bungalow. In the meantime I found out many things about her. She was seven years older than me, a fact which had not been made known to me. She was well experienced, having worked in London before the war as a maid. Apparently the butlers in the big houses would make the maids see to their wishes. If she did not he would most probably dismiss them on some fictitious charge and as jobs were hard to find the girls more often than not had to see to the butler's wishes. We had a disagreement and she decided to go back home again at a minute's notice.

It turned out for the best in the end, because if I had married her I am quite sure that it would have made things very difficult for me, her wanting to go out gadding about and having so many friends. Of course, I would never have met my dear good wife, with whom I eventually spent sixty perfectly happy years.

Later on when we had to move depots, the Sergeant who had been kidding my girlfriend had to ride with me on my FWD wagon which I used for first aid. I thought to myself, now is the time that I will get my own back on him. We had to sit right over the top of the radiator which was very high off the ground and, of course, the earth came rushing up. It did not go very fast, it would only do about 20 mph all out, but we came to a very steep hill and I put it into neutral to coast downwards. I should not have done this, of course, and as we were flying along he was gripping the seat for grim death and I said to him that the brakes were no good on these vehicles, which they weren't, of course. In the end we were going so fast I even got the wind up myself as I just could not hold it back. Luckily we were on a very straight run and we were able to stop. I think we must have been doing about 60 mph in the end and he got a real fright. Nevertheless, I gained some pleasure out of knowing that I had just got my own back.

Myself and six other lads were sent to Scotland from a mobilisation centre and we joined a company in Edinburgh; it must have been October. Whilst we were in London we had been going around in our shirt sleeves but when we got to Edinburgh, having travelled through the night, it was terribly cold and we had to put on our greatcoats immediately we got off the train. There was a peculiar noise under the roadway which we just could not understand, but when daylight came we could see that it was an underground cable which had hauled the trams along, much as they do in San Francisco even today. Eventually we saw the power house where there were miles of cables and drums and the cables were a terrific length due to the fact that there were no extra pick up points, but the trams would only go very slowly. You could, in fact, see elderly men running and jumping onto the trams as they were going at full speed and one good feature was that you were able to travel from one end of Edinburgh to the other which was indeed quite a long way for only sixpence.

I can remember one time going up to a place which they called King Arthur's Seat. This was a hill just outside Edinburgh and it really was a treat to see so much of the Scottish countryside round about. In the distance you were able to see the steam from trains puffing along and we were able to gain an excellent view. The company to which we had been sent had numerous peerless wagons. These wagons wre American and belonged to the Canadian Forestry Corps which had come over from Canada and which was made up of lumberjacks. They had been put to work on the extensive timber forest in Scotland. These fellows were very undisciplined. They did not salute officers or even say 'Sir'. They had 9 hp Indian motor bikes which were very powerful. One day our OC came into the garage and saw one of these motor bikes and decided that he would like to have a ride upon it so he climbed on the bike and kick-started it. There was no stand so you had to leave one foot on the floor to balance and as soon as he put the bike into gear he did not realise what a powerful engine it had and it shot forward and collided with a concrete sand pit. Fortunately he was not badly hurt, but it did upset him rather.

One time I was working on one of the wagons which had to be completely overhauled. I had it jacked up and there was something wrong with the gearbox. I had the lid off and was looking to see if I could find out what the trouble was when the OC came along with one or two of the high-ranking staff officers. They saw this gearbox opened and our Sergeant asked me to start up the engine, which I did, and they stood looking at the gearbox and then the Sergeant said, 'Rev it up'. I told him that if I revved it up the grease would fly out. He said, 'Never mind, they want to see it accelerating'. Reluctantly I accelerated and, of course, the grease flew out all over them and I felt terrible! Nevertheless, I had only been obeying the Sergeant's instructions.

We had a big tank which was was lit by a fire. The water was heated up and all the engine pieces were then placed in to enable them to be degreased. We had a cat and it had kittens and I can remember that somebody drowned the kittens by putting them in this boiling hot water. One of the lady drivers which we had at that time saw this and reported it to the OC. Of course he had to do something about this incident so he placed a notice that whoever had done this had to come forward. Of course nobody came forward so then the OC stopped all leave and all late passes.

I became very friendly with the Staff Sergeant in the works there. I knew my job and he would give me all the important jobs to do. I was put on a draft to go to Ireland and he came up to me and said, 'I see you are on this draft for Ireland'. I said, 'Yes, I'm pleased about it', so he said, 'I don't know why you should be pleased about it, do you want shooting in the back?' I said, 'Well, not particularly'. In the meantime I was put on another draft to go back down to London to our mob centre to be sent overseas. I was recalled as I was not of age. Syd Wyatt was amongst the lads that went over to France and after about a fortnight I received a postcard from my brother to say that Syd and a few of the other lads had been working on a lorry which had been a direct hit and they were all blown to smithereens. They were never found; there was no trace of their bodies. I thought to myself that this must have been a let off for me as if I had gone to France with the original lads, it may well have been me that had come to such a sticky end. It seemed to me that this was another incident where I thought that somebody was looking after me.

One night two or three of us decided to go up into the city. I remember that we wanted to go to either the cinema or the theatre. On our way into the city we passed a row of houses. A little old lady pulled the curtains to one side in one of the houses and waved frantically at us. We went into the house thinking that she was in some sort of trouble, but when we went in this dimly lit hall she took us into the front room and there were three girls partially dressed. It turned out to be a brothel so we simply beat a hasty retreat.

We came across a theatre and outside there was a picture of an aeroplane. I thought to myself that this would suit me in any case, no matter what the play was about. We had a quick lunch of sandwiches and we joined the queue at about 2 o'clock. At 7.00 pm we were still in the queue. People would queue all afternoon for the night show. During the afternoon we had seen several buskers and we had given them coppers every now and again as they passed. The play was called *The Arcadians* and in it they had a mock aeroplane on the stage. There was a comedian whose name was Billy Merson and he sang a song entitled 'I've got a motto, always merry and bright'. This had been the song that I had sung at our army concerts.

Whilst we were in the theatre there was an air raid and we had to leave and walk the eightmiles to get back to our billets. Bombs and shrapnel were dropping all about us. There was a terrific blast and I lost my hat. I also got a splinter in one of my eyes, it was very painful and when I arrived back at the camp I was taken off to the hospital. I was in the military hospital for almost three weeks where they managed to remove the splinter from my eye. I was again very lucky indeed because at the military hospital there had been an eye specialist, very unusual at that time.

Whilst at the RASC MT Headquarters in London, a notice was posted that somebody was needed, preferably an ex-cinema operator, to show films. I applied and I thought to myself that if I got the job I would be there for quite some time. I did get the job but as I was going to the cinema with the Sergeant, he said to me, 'Oh, I see that you are on draft'. I did not know about this but when I looked at the orders, I was indeed on draft again. I was very disappointed to miss this job.

Later when I was visiting some of the depots where our wagons were stationed, I came to a place which had three hospitals with nothing but VD patients. Each had five hundred beds and at this particular time there were more soldiers laid up with VD than were in fact wounded. I went into the Sergeant's office and said, 'My goodness, what an awful smell!' and he said, 'Yes, they are the dead houses next door'. 'Do they die from it?' I asked. 'Oh yes'. was the reply. He then described how some of them died. When I joined up I did not know anything about VD or any of the other things. One evening whilst we were having our meal the MO came around and was lecturing to us about the perils of VD and it most definitely put me off going with strange girls.

One day whilst I was working the Sergeant came to me and said, 'I've got a job for you, I want you to go and pick up a couple of prisoners'. I enquired about the Provost Sergeant as this was his job. The Sergeant made some excuse but, of course, it was an order so I had to go. I had known that these two lads had been in France and had been wounded two or three times and they just did not care twopence for anybody.

They had taken one of the army wagons and had driven off. They had run out of petrol at Northampton and eventually they had been caught without any passes. I told the Sergeant Major that I knew these two lads and thought that I had better have an armed escort.

'Oh you won't want that,' he said.

'Well how about handcuffs then?' I asked.

'No you'll be alright'. So off we went to the jail to pick them up. We went in a small van and when we arrived we were informed that they had 'sloped off'. It was very early in the morning so I said to my lads, 'Come on, we'll go and have some breakfast'. We hunted round for a café and eventually came across one and, lo and behold, these two lads were sitting having egg and bacon. They said to me, 'Hello Percy, have you come for us'? 'Yes', I said. 'Well we are not coming'. We all had breakfast and eventually I was able to pursuade them to go and get their kit bags. However, we had about 25 miles to travel and when we came within a mile or two of the camp the lads asked me to stop as they wanted to hide some cigarettes in their boots. They took off their boots and put the cigarettes inside and I said, 'No, I can't stop. You are not supposed to do that'. They were all but drunk – we found out later that they had had a bottle of whisky with them in their kit bags. When I said that I could not stop, one of the lads took out a razor which was the old open type from the kit bag and said, 'I'll cut your throat if you don't stop'. So I told our lads that the only thing we could do was to try and overpower them and tie them up with our putties. I said, 'Take your putties off'. In the meantime the two lads were lolling about in the back of the van but they thought better of it and we managed to get them back to the camp. When they came up for trial the powers that be were so afraid of these two lads that they got off almost scot free.

When we were billeted in Hitchin, there was a barber's shop there and we would go for a shave. There was a father and his lovely daughter. The daughter used to give us such a lovely gentle shave. It was amusing to see the fellows waiting to be shaved. They would watch to see whose turn it was and when it was the girl's turn (when the father was busy cutting or whatever) they would say, 'Go on, I am not in a hurry'. It really was amusing to see how they would try and get the girl to shave them because she really did give you a nice gently shave.

One time when I was home on leave one of the jobs I had was to overhaul one of the fire escapes for the local Corporation. My father asked me to take old Rave with me, as he was a good painter and liner. My father asked me would I go down with him and extend a fire escape so that he would be able to paint and varnish it. Whenever I came home on leave old Rave would say to me, 'Christ, haven't they shot you yet?' and I would say to him 'Blimey, are you not dead yet?' He would never tell us his age and I would say to him, 'I'll find out how old you are, I'll come and have a look on your gravestone'. He would only laugh. Actually he was 84 when he died but he was a grand old chap. He could take a joke and give a joke and he was a marvellous workman. Eventually he graded to making buses and coaches when the wheelwrighting era was practically over and he became quite adept at this.

One of the army bikes we had was a 1912 vintage. We had a BSA and also a Triumph. We later had some Scot and Squirrels, which were twin-cylinder two-stroke engines and water cooled and they were very reliable bikes. Of course, they were very low and we played tricks with these on the lorry park when nobody was looking. One of the things we did was to put one hand out on to the ground and use a pivet and roll around in circles and being very low it had no top bar on. There was plenty of leg room in it and we were able to rear them up on the rear wheels and drive like that. We later had some quite reliable Harley Davidson bikes and also some little two and three quarter Douglas bikes and four horse Douglas bikes which were twin cylinder horizontal opposed and I loved these, especially the four horse model.

I can remember one time an officer and I took out a convoy and when we were on our way back, we had about 30 or 40 miles to do. The officer said to me, 'Come on Sergeant, we'll have a race back to the depot'. We set off, he on a little two and three quarter Douglas and me on the heavier Triumph. I had to slow down because I had a job to keep seated on a very rough patch. Of course he came flying past me and then when we reached a good level piece of macadam road I would accelerate and go flying past him. I can see him now, his coat tails flapping up as he passed me. Of course, you were not supposed to pass an Officer, but he did not mind.

When it came time for my demob, it was just before Christmas and I was asked if I would like to sign on for another period. They said that they would make me a Mechanical Sergeant Major and place me in charge of the works. I would have been given very good pay but I told them that I was sorry but I had a business to go home to. Eventually I obtained my papers, but unfortunately they had to be signed by an officer or a warrant officer. I took my papers to the warrant officer on duty and asked him if he would sign my papers. He said, 'Well what is it worth, is it worth a double whisky?' I did not like this form of blackmail but nevertheless I did it as it meant that I could go home that night instead of having to wait until the next morning. I came home on leave for Christmas and theoretically I was discharged but I did not have the final papers so needless to say I was not too fussy about going back on time. When I eventually returned to camp the Sergeant Major put me on the peg right away for being absent without leave.

Before long, however, I was home permanently in Southport again, working in civvy street and free, at last, of all the orders, discipline and strict life of the army.

Chapter Seven

The Mannings of Birkdale

IT IS AMAZING how the coastline around Southport has changed since I was very young. The sea is encroaching and the whole area of the sandhills has altered. There used to be some tremendously tall sandhills in my younger days and we had some rare old fun jumping up and down them. There was also quite a big area of marsh land which we called the slacks. It is now the golf links and it was always full of very interesting wildlife. We used to go down there with jam jars and look for tadpoles or frogs which were there in abundance. We would look for birds nests and it was lovely to lie on our backs and watch the skylark climb up into the sky and hover above, whistling and singing so beautifully, but you never see anything like this now. I sometimes walk up there but sadly there are no skylarks to be seen at all. I suppose it is due to all the insecticides which are used and which have probably killed them all off.

When my sons and I used to go fishing, we would dig holes for what we called lug worms. These left a cast on the top of the sand and you had to use a very narrow spade to dig down very quickly because if you were not quick enough digging down slant-wise the worms would be gone. We used these worms as bait on a long line which had several hooks on it and we would anchor them down at very low tide. When the tide had gone out again we would go and pick up the fish.

The sea used to get very rough and I liked to go down to the pier and fish with lines. I went down one Easter Monday and I lost about four lines through the crabs taking the bait off the hooks. Sometimes the hooks would get tangled up in wreckage or in the bottom of the pier irons and when you came to haul them in the line would break and you would lose all your tackle. On this particular Monday I sat there all day and at one time the waves were washing over the pier and I did not catch a bite. At other times I have seen people land conger eels as much as five or six feet long and as thick as your wrist, but you had to be very careful not to be bitten by one. Later on a couple of steamships were wrecked out on the Horsebank and as they gradually went into ruin it was a good source for catching conger eels because they lived in the wrecks. I think there are still some parts of the wrecks there to this day.

If you went along the beach as far as Freshfield you were able to see some marvellous shipping; and you could see ships of all sizes coming and going all day and night, but alas you hardly see one now.

During the last war quite a few ships were torpedoed or struck mines in the channel and I can remember one ship which had been loaded with sewing machines and cases of whisky. There were literally thousands of cases of whisky and as the ship broke up the cases floated ashore. People went down to collect them and take them away until the Customs heard about this and came and left watchmen on the roads leading from the beach. I have known lads go down and pick up these cases, dig a hole and bury them and then go back later on to pick them up. They were able to sell the whisky at a very good price.

On June 29th, 1927, there was a total eclipse and my family went down to see this. One of the vantage points was the 'Round House' (a remarkable building built in 1925), in Waterloo Road. At the very same time there was an aeroplane which was setting off to fly back across the Atlantic. As it was being refuelled the tyres were sinking into the sand. They had to get some wooden sleepers and make a sort of bed for it. When it finally took off it didn't even bother to circle, it just set off straight away for America where I understand it landed safely.

There were two other shipwrecks which I remember. One was the three-masted Irish schooner *Happy Harry* with a three-man crew, and the other was the pilot boat *Charles Livingston*. The schooner ran into a gale which blew all its sails into tatters and it eventually ran aground and the crew abandoned it. On the following tide it floated itself and was washing down towards the pier. In fact, I saw it as it eventually collided with, and lodged into, the pier. Somebody went out in a duck (which was an ex-army amphibian). It was very rough but they managed to get a line aboard and pull it clear of the pier and they were then able to beach it. Eventually they set it alight – it was a wooden hull so it burned well. They placed a lot of shavings and inflammable materials around it and, as the hull had been pitched so many times, it became a roaring furnace.

In 1939, the pilot boat got lost in the darkness as the crew had thought that they were off the Welsh coast when in fact they were off the Lancashire coast. They were eventually grounded and, sadly, 23 lives were lost. They were so near the beach that they could have simply walked back, but apparently the water was so cold that they only lasted a few minutes. Only ten of the crew were saved by clinging to the rigging until the tide went down and then they were able to be brought ashore. Spectacular, but very sad.

The fishermen used to put down nets five or six feet deep in a huge circle and when the tide came in the fish got caught in the nets and when the tide went out they were then able to take the fish out and take them home to be sold. One Sunday I was down there after a terrific thunderstorm which they used to say drove the mackerel ashore. The fishermen were selling the mackerel at 24 for one shilling, but there was such a glut that they could not get rid of them all.

We would go treading for cockles and we would take off our boots and socks and proceed very slowly along a given track and the cockles would come out. It was just a question of picking them up and taking them home, washing them, salting them and then we would cook them. Nowadays, I understand, they simply rake the cockle beds with rakes towed behind tractors. The same applies to shrimps; they go out with a tractor or modern 'rig' with a stove on board and catch the shrimps and cook them as they trawl for more. It is not, however, quite the industry it one was.

The factory in Kew Road, Birkdale, opposite our house was built at the beginning of the century as a scrapyard for a local marine store dealer. At the top of the building there was quite a big room which my father rented and formed a working mens and boys club. Eventually he was able to buy four billiard tables and people derived a great deal of pleasure from these.

We had various whist drives and beetle drives to provide funds to help with the expenses and people made hot-pots and I can remember climbing the stairs, which are there to this day, with a huge hot-pot which my mother had made in a big stone jar; this was nearly eighty years ago. Sadly when war broke out the club was disbanded and the building had various uses since then.

In the same yard was a carpet beating firm and they made a terrific noise with their gas engine which drove a lot of big beaters. They would place the carpet in the machine and set it in motion. The beaters moved the carpet around and it was surprising to see just how much dust it would get out.

In the 1920s the Southport Motor Club began racing cars and motorbikes on the beach. There were also one or two speed attempts. I can remember Henry Segrave being down there one time with a Sunbeam and turning in a speed of over 200 miles an hour. In 1926 he grabbed the world record at 160 m.p.h. Other attemps were made by Malcolm Campbell, Jack Field and Earl Howe, in 1928. There was a local gentleman who asked me to make an aluminium tail and fit it to his racing car for when he was turning at very high speeds the car would swerve about and would become almost out of control. I made this for him, which helped to correct the swerving but it was never a real success. At one meeting May Cunliffe and her father entered a Sunbeam open tourer. It was a very well made car and they set off in one of the races. After they had done a few laps the sand was getting banked up on the corners. She went into one corner too fast and the car rolled over and pinned her father down by the neck; it was very unfortunate that the backrest landed on his neck killing him instantly.

During 1910 my father and two friends from the church bought shares in a small coalmine in Skelmersdale, the idea being to sell coal at a very reasonable rate to poor people. The coal, which was shallow mined, burned very hot but left a lot of ash which the average housewife would not tolerate. It was decided to see if there was a market among the poorer people for cheap coal and indeed there was a lot of interest. Don't forget, in those days a fire had to be lit before you could even boil a kettle and most bedrooms had coal fires in them, so quite a lot of coal was used.

The next problem was one of how to get the coal from Skelmersdale to Southport and a firm called Taskers in the south made tractors, one of which was bought by the coalmine. It was steam-engined, rated at 4h.p., with solid iron wheels, all brass and steel. A strong wire cable drum was attached to one of its rear wheel hubs and was used to extricate itself or other vehicles which were stuck and it was very useful for uprooting trees. It also had a canopy big enough for one person. For such a small engine it had quite a large water tank, and a long suction pipe to pump water, very often from a ditch or hydrant. It also had two little paraffin lamps, which had a habit of going out at every pothole! It was eventually driven by road to Southport and then came the problem of where to start it up.

A pair of houses in Kew Road, with two large entrances and stables at the back, were bought. I don't know where they kept getting the money from, as my father had only his coachbuilding, wheelwright and smithy. They must have had some good backers who had confidence in them.

Some 12 x 12 baulks of pitch pine were bought from the old aerial flight (taken down 1911) which crossed the lake at Southport, together with a staging and covering which was made to hold the coal in bags, and also the bags of sawdust which were brought from Liverpool and which were eventually sold to the pubs and the butchers.

Next came the problem of trailers – Taskers' were very well made but expensive, so, instead, father obtained three second-hand ex-Liverpool horse drawn wagons which carried about 12 tons. He fitted new tow bars instead of the shafts and sideboards and it was decided to carry the coal loose and bag it at this end. Three horse-drawn coal lorries were made and painted, lined and lettered, and they were very smart indeed. Obviously the coal bags had to be treated and waterproofed and fitted with metal tags to show their exact weight. Three lots of scales had to be certified that they were measuring correctly.

Three horses were brought from Liverpool. One was a beautiful six year old but sadly it went lame and had to be destroyed. Another was called Dobbin. He was like a huge waterbutt on four legs and he proved to be a disaster. He had only been used to plodding around the docks and when the driver began to deliver the coal Dobbin would go where he wanted and no amount of persuading would lead him down the right road. I can remember one Sunday morning I was riding our own pony down to the beach when my elder brother took him from me and told me to go and get Dobbin. With a struggle, I eventually climbed upon his massive back but after a short while I think he decided that he did not want to go and get his feet wet so he turned around and headed for home. Sadly we had to let Dobbin go.

The third horse was Sandy; he was a loveable giant of a horse. It would appear that Sandy's first driver had been a small man with a vicious temper. Sandy had spent most of his time on the hard road at the docks and he just could not understand why he could not get going on the soft cinders. I think he thought that the skids were under the wheels and he was waiting for them to be moved.

Fred, who was a conscientious, middle-aged, clay-pipe smoker and traction engine driver, took charge of Sandy. He loved horses as much as he loved engines. I remember he asked me if I would like to go to Skelmersdale with him to take an empty trailer. Of course I jumped at the chance. We sat chatting away and eventually we came upon Heathy Lane Bridge. It was quite a pull up and half way up Sandy stopped. I thought for one awful moment that the trailer was about to roll backwards. Not so; Sandy simply turned right and let the front wheel roll back into the gutter and he stood on three legs and rested. When he was good and ready he moved on without being told to do so.

This made both Fred and myself very apprehensive about approaching the old Red Lion bridge. In those days it was a hump-back bridge and took no more than one vehicle at a time and it was very steep indeed. I said, 'I am very worried about going down the Red Lion bridge, Fred.' 'I'm only worried about going up,' said Fred. Neither of us need have worried ourselves, because Sandy struggled up and as soon as he reached the peak he stopped so that a chain could be put on the wheels to hold it back. Next were the old waterworks and the road on either side going up was made from flint cobbles. Of course, the road to Ormskirk was notoriously narrow and very busy. We duly arrived at the

Skelmersdale mine, unharnessed Sandy, gave him his nosebag, much to his appreciation, and Fred and myself sat by a huge heap of coal and had our bread, cheese and cold tea.

Next came the long twelve miles home with no trailer, of course. Sandy followed us without the lead rein, no doubt thinking how nice his straw bed would be when he eventually got home. I learned a lot about country life - haymaking, wild flowers, animals and birds - on that long walk home.

A name had to be found for the coal mine and it was called Mutual Benefit Coal Supply and Carrier Company. This name was painted on the canopy of the engine. A driver was appointed but he proved to be very unsatisfactory. He was an American and he nearly ruined the little giant in the very first month. He had tied the governors up in order to increase the speed, sucking up dirty water which meant dropping plugs, rattling the whole engine and causing the tubes to leak and very often he would break down in the country, so he was dismissed.

Father asked Fred if he would be prepared to take over as driver, together with my brother as his second man. This worked very well for quite a while and sometimes my brother would let me have a go at the wheel. I was enchanted by this and I was also very observant. One day he left me on the footplate in the roadway whilst he went to get some cigarettes. I had seen him pull a little lever to let out a cloud of hissing steam. I thought that I would give this a try. Unfortunately a laundry van came past at the same time and the horse showed a good clean boot.

A little brass spring loaded knob fascinated me but I hadn't seen it being used. I thought it best to leave well alone, but one day my brother was pulling up a big oak tree on his own. The winch cable and chain were placed around the bottom of the trunk, big baulks of timber scotched the wheels and the brake was hard on, the throttle opened and there was a terrific heave. The roots were long and heavy and this is where the little brass knob came in. My brother asked me up and told me to press it. I had to use both my hands but what an upheaval. The engine bucked and reared and after much rending and tearing of wood, the mighty oak gave in. The little knob let high pressure steam into the low pressure cylinder thereby giving a tremendous surge of power.

A firm in Southport called C. F. Chinnery's, housed at Pavilion Buildings, Lord Street, from 1894 to 1931, were furniture removers and had several big pantechnicon vans. They also had a little giant exactly like ours, but with extra tanks mounted on the side of the boilers. When they were busy they would hire our engine.

From here on things began to deteriorate. The mine, I think, became waterlogged and worked out. The little giant was taken over by the army and taken to France.

My brother had earned some money delivering groceries with the little pony and cart on Saturday mornings. He used some of his money to buy an old motorbike called Minerva. It had a 3 h.p. engine with a battery in the tank which provided low tension ignition and had a fixed engine. It had no gearbox or clutch and you had to run quite quickly, press a lever which lifted the exhaust valve to let you get going, and as soon as you dropped the lever, theoretically the engine should have started, but of course, it did not always do this.

One time my brother let me have a ride. I rode to the corner and turned without stopping but I had to lean over at a tremendous angle. I did not come off, but when I got back to the group of boys, my brother said, "One of these days you will come off turning round like that." Later he managed to buy a sidecar which was of the old open type. It was almost like a bath chair made out of wicker. Of course the passenger would have to help to push start it. When the engine started they had to climb in over the back of the sidecar. Being a fixed engine the Minerva was very limited. You couldn't go up any hills, and I can remember coming across a flock of sheep and, not wanting to let the engine stop, I went rather quickly through them and unfortunately banged into a few of them which upset me very much.

We had a lot of fun with this little motor bike, but eventually he changed it for another one called a Puegot which had a variable speed pulley. It did not have a clutch or gearbox, you had to operate a lever which opened the pulley, but the belt used to be very slack and it would slip. This had a low tension battery, so we thought about fixing a high tension magneto on the engine. By putting an extension on one of the shafts which drove the exhaust valves and putting a sprocket on it, we drove the magneto by chain round the sprocket. It was only a very 'gerry' set up and very often the chain would come off and the engine would stop. We got used to timing it and putting the chain back on again so that we no longer had to take the plug out to see where the piston was. We just pushed it to get it on full compression and then slipped the cover off the magneto and watched where the points opened. We would then put the chain on and invariably we got it right.

At the beginning of 1915, my brother volunteered to join the army and he went to Manchester. He left his motorbike there for me to pick up. I went on the train and father went on his bicycle. We stayed with a friend overnight and the next day we set off for home. Father put a rope to the back of the motorbike and he held on to it. He was pedalling at the same time so as not to get entangled in the rope. We managed to get to Wigan before the engine gave out. I looked down at the chain on the magneto and saw that it wasn't turning. Something had gone wrong inside the compartment where the gear wheels were, which worked the valves, so of course, not having any tools or spares I had to do the rest of the journey by train. However, father finished the journey quite safely and when I came to take the timing cover off I discovered that a nut had dropped off the lever which controlled the half compression device for easy starting, and it had fallen amongst the gear wheels and stripped them. That was the reason why the engine would not go, but the motorbike was quite reliable for an old stager.

During the time when I helped to show pictures, I had an Enfield motorbike and one night one of the girls asked if she could have a ride back home. I had never tried taking anybody on the back before as it had very narrow handlebars and it was rather difficult to control. However, she got on and sat side-saddle. I went round the block wobbling quite a bit, but alas, as we came back to the picture palace we were looking at some of the girls standing in the doorway, and as I turned a sharp corner there was a terrific clanging of a bell. When I quickly turned round and looked, I was heading straight for a tramcar. Luckily I swerved and narrowly avoided a collision.

Before the talkies came out they had a pianist playing the piano as the pictures were silent and had sub-titles. The films were changed three nights a week and on each of these nights a great big fat lady would come with a little lady who would sit behind her. The big lady either could not read or could not see, I don't know which, but the little lady used to read out all the sub-titles and sometimes somebody would shout 'Shut up' because they could not concentrate on the film which more often than not would be a series.

One was called 'Pearl White', and week after week this series went on. It always ended up at an exciting point with the heroine being tied up on a saw bench which would start up and gradually make its way towards a circular saw. Of course, the hero always came along just at the right time and switched it off.

Then there was the 'Pathe Gazette', which had the news twice a week. It was quite something when they eventually brought out the talkies. I remember one of the cinemas in the town was called the Picturedrome. Built in 1910, it later became the Forum. The manager was very go-ahead and he tried to match the picture with the record. On one occasion when he was showing John Peel in a film, and John Peel was on a horse in hunting gear, he set the record up but he could not get it to match perfectly.

Wilfred, my brother, became a projectionist and showed the very first talking picture in Southport, which starred Al Jolson, at the Empire (later Scala). The sound was on a big record and they had two projectors and the operator had to change quickly from one machine to the other without having to switch off or disrupt the picture. My brother was very good at this and the audience never realised the film and record had been changed.

The Winter Gardens in Southport were very nice and it was a great shame when it was all taken away. Unfortunately, the main buildings disappeared at the start of the 1930s. It consisted of an area of lovely landscaped gardens, flower beds, a theatre, a zoo and an aquarium. There was a glass-covered causeway leading to the other end and a building which was used as a skating rink. There was seating down both sides of the building and quite a lot of space so that when it was raining people could go in and listen to the orchestra playing.

When the first moving pictures came to the theatre, I took my younger brother along one night. It was in the very early stages of projection, and the film was actually running into a basket just underneath the machine which had to be rewound, which was very, very dangerous because there was no projection box. There was also a big corrugated iron building which was used as a circus, and I can remember being there one night when there was a terrific thunderstorn and the hail was battering down on to the roof and I was very frightened. Later on this became Woodhead's garage, The Motorhouse in 1908, Whiteside's (1924), Kirby's. I remember seeing one of the very first Model T Fords taxis plying for trade outside. I think it was 1911 and that particular driver and a friend set up a business in the town specialising in repairing Model T. Fords. It was a mighty queer-looking thing, the first taxi. I remember the rear wings floated straight out of the back and they did not follow the curvature of the wheels. Of course, that was when they first started making them in Trafford Park, Manchester.

It is easy, when looking back in one's life, to refer to 'the good old days'. But when you really think about it, not everything was better then. Can you imaging having live maggots placed on a wound to suck out the poison, and can you imagine having a halfpenny spending money on a Saturday morning? We used to value this halfpenny and buy the maximum amount of sweets or popcorn or whatever. Money for tram fares was not given out unless the weather was very, very bad, or for some other reason. We were expected to walk into town and think nothing of it.

Discipline was the main thing. Most men wore leather straps as well as braces, and if the father of the family was seen to start to unbuckle his belt, somebody could expect a thrashing. This did not apply in our case as our father did not wear a belt; nevertheless there was always a cane hanging from a picture in the corner. I only remember this being used once on me and this was when I had been sent outside to look after my younger brother who was in his pram. I was hanging on to the pram handle and upset the pram. Luckily, my brother was strapped in and he did not fall out. My father gave me such a whacking to remind me to to do this again. Another time I got a ticking off was for walking along the top of a wall when I should not have been and I tore the trousers of my Sunday best suit.

I was once given four strokes on my hand for playing truant. I'll never forget it to my dying day and I often think what a good thing it was to have corporal punishment.

As regards discipline at school, every morning the headmaster would line us up and make sure that we had a clean face, neck and hands and that our shoes had been cleaned. Dress wasn't as important because they knew that a lot of people could not afford to keep having new suits, but they realised that by having a little bit of soap and shoe polish you were able to keep yourself respectable.

All the teachers had a cane which they used at their descretion. Possibly if you had not learned your lesson properly or you were found talking, or if you had not written neatly. If the teacher decided that you were to have the cane, you had it. Occasionally, an irate parent, nearly always a mother would come to the school and complain to the headmaster. It did not make the slightest difference as the headmaster himself was quite a tough guy and he could put up with all the abuse and, no doubt about it, it was a good school which produced good results so there must have been something that worked in their format.

As regards games, we used to play in the playground, football, skipping and leapfrog and in the winter we would make a slide and generally we were very active. At night we used to play games with our grandparents in the house. The most popular were drafts, ludo and snakes and ladders. Nowadays, of course, it's computers and electronic games and other expensive things. I don't think, however, that the children derive as much pleasure out of these, for they soon seem to tire of them, whereas we would make things last for a long time.

Chapter Eight

Civvy Motoring and Marriage

IN THE EARLY DAYS of motoring, before the plate clutches were very popular, there was what they called a 'cone clutch' which was made at an angle. It was lined with leather and eventually this leather would wear down. You would then have to re-line the clutch. You had to cut a piece of leather, possibly two and a half to three inches wide, and cut it into a semi-circular shape, according to the angle. It would then have to be rivetted on to the clutch with copper rivets and then filed if there were any ridges.. Otherwise, when you came to use the clutch, until it had worn itself level they were very fierce. This was quite an operation - you had to disconnect the drive from the engine to the gear box.

The gear box was a separate unit engine and there was a shaft in between, sometimes with a universal coupling which had to be unbolted and disconnected. Also, if you had an engine out for any reason, it all had to be lined up again in the chassis, being a separate unit from the gear box, as if there was not a universal joint between the engine and the gear box. Eventually you would get metal fatigue and the shaft would ultimately shear off. No mechanic would understand how to do this these days. You had to fix a pointer and clip it onto the shaft and run it round the outside of the flywheel to get the right depth on the engine brackets, then run it round the face of the flywheel to make sure that it was in line and in a horizontal plane. The same thing applied when scraping any bearings on the connecting rods. You had to line the connecting rods up to make sure they were at right angles to the crankshaft and in a vertical plane, otherwise there would be a lot of excess friction on the pistons. Daimler engines had this system and the sleeve was operated by little connecting rods, so that you had to remetal the big ends on the connecting rods and also a little connecting rod to each sleeve. If it was a six cylinder engine, that meant there were 12 of these little rods and they were all white metal. They had to be scraped to be fitted and then plumbed up vertically. There again, the present day mechanic would not have the slightest idea of how to do any of these things.

We had a 1907 Rolls Royce chassis for sale. This was a very old model and we found out that there had only been three of this particular model made. A gentleman from Halifax, who made gasometers, heard that it was for sale and thought that if he had a Rolls Royce wagon he would have a good show. He intended to buy the chassis and have a lorry body built on it. Rolls Royce got to know about this and they themselves bought it because they did not want Rolls Royce to be seen with a lorry body on.

At our Chapel we had a very go-ahead Minister. He formed what they called the Youth Club Good Companions. Eventually, my wife and my mother decided to try and make some funds for the Sunday School by producing concerts. I used to write out a script, usually in the form of a pantomime. We had well over 20 in the Youth Club. Incidentally, a lot of them kept together and some eventually married and are still together. It just goes to show how a good beginning at the chapel led to better things.

My wife and mother made the costumes for them. We put on some very attractive shows and I used to write funny pieces into them. It was really lovely for me hearing the children laughing at the different episodes. One time I borrowed a pantomime horse and put my two boys in it. One at the front and one at the rear. My youngest boy, who was only four at the time was dressed as Little Lord Fauntleroy. He had been taught some lines to say, but during the course of the performance he forgot them. I could see my eldest son's face in the horse's mouth and he was trying to tell his younger brother what to say. It was rather a funny experience.

I became involved in this and on one occasion I was dressed as a baby and I was pushed around the stage. I had made a dummy into a sort of whistle and every now and again I would blow the dummy which whistled and caused tremendous laughter. The title of my song was 'I ain't nobody's baby,' which I had to sing eventually.

A few of the older people did not think that it was the right thing to have these hilarious happenings in the Sunday School, but it gave such a lot of happiness to the families who came.

We sometimes had to repeat the concerts as people just could not get in, and we made as much as £25 in one night for the Sunday School funds, which in 1942 was a considerable sum.

One of my sons had gone to some of trouble to make the stage even more presentable. He had put footlights on and a couple of limelights. One night as we were rehearsing, the Sunday School superintendent came in and asked us if we needed all the lights. We could not understand why. Of course, he was quite right in asking as it was his job to keep expenses down. I explained to him that it all helped to make the concert a success and he appreciated this. The idea was that we would sing a popular song and I would sing out of tune. I would have about four children on the stage with me and each time I sang out of tune I would blame each one of the children.

One time we did a very ambitious scene. I forget now what it was called, but in it my eldest son was dressed as a knight. He had made himself a suit of armour and I had provided him with some thin metal to make a breast plate and a sword. I made the boots for him in my smithy because they were difficult for him to make. He needed chain mail armour for the outfit and my mother knitted some out of string and we sprayed it with aluminium and it looked very effective.

The name of our firm was W. Manning, Wheelwright, Coachbuilder, Blacksmiths and it was changed a few years later to W. Manning and Sons and later still became W. Manning and Sons Limited. We became known as Motor Agents, Engineers, Coach Proprietors. In the year 1923 we were agents for an American vehicle called a Traffic, which was a solid-tyred, two-tonne vehicle and it had a peculiar drive. It did not have a normal floating type, it was driven by pinions working inside the hub. The hub was in the form of a gear wheel and it was a system of gear reduction, but the oiling system was very poor. We had two in stock and the prices were reduced £500 overnight. Of course, we had no hopes of getting this back by selling the vehicles, so my father said, 'Oh well, we'll put coach bodies on because it is beginning to be the coach era.' So we put coach bodies on them and then we had a smaller chassis which was made into a 14-seater coach and it was called a Greyhound.

My brothers and I were each put to driving these coaches in the first year. I hated having to drive the coach especially with any drunken parties. I didn't mind so much going out with say, a Sunday school outing or bowling club. I thoroughly hated this particular period of my working life which continued for several years. We were building the coaches and the buses in the winter and in the summertime we were running them.

What I didn't like, of course, was when they broke down, especially when we had started running the long distance coaches. I might just be going out to the pictures or somewhere with my wife and the telephone would ring and somebody would say, 'I've got a big end gone,' and I would say, 'Where are you?' It could have been in Devonshire or on the way to London or anywhere. Of course, I had to get a suitable vehicle and go and make arrangements for the passengers to get home. I would go and tow the coach home having travelled overnight in the

The second barrel organ I built, which has been donated to the Imperial Cancer Research Fund for use in Scotland.

The author, Percy Manning.

The cause of it all, Walter Chamberlain Manning, my father.

My family and myself touring Norfolk in an early, 20-horsepower Vulcan.

The grandfather clock, made by myself, for one of my grandsons – note the 'working' blacksmiths at the top of the clock, which strike an anvil as the clock chimes.

One of my youngest son's outdoor exhibits at the Southport Flower Show, for which he awarded all the major prizes. It consisted of a red-brick and mortar building and a working waterwheel, complete with working lock gates that I made for him during my retirement. I made several things each year and enjoyed working on the exhibits.

What a normal coach party looked like in the early 1920s. Note, in particular, the hats which everyone invariably wore. This would probably be on a journey to Blackpool which in those days cost 5 shillings return for a full day's outing.

Setting off for London, 1926. This was the trial run for the first long-distance outings which we pioneered. At that time it cost £1 return for two full days in London. I am the driver here – and a rather unwilling one at that!

One of the first purpose-built motor caravans, designed and made by my father in 1920. He used steam-bent 2in x 1in English ash for the framework and the newly introduced big sheets of plywood, which made the body both light and strong. A unique layout of sleeping arrangements gave six berths, with a dividing screen if required.

I overhauled the chassis, a 1912 Belsize 20-horsepower, and put on stronger rear wheels, with detachable rings, and extra leaves in the rear springs. New tyres were fitted all round. We did not carry spare wheels but never had a puncture in all the miles we covered all over England and Wales.

There weren't any electrics, only paraffin side- and tail-lamps and a bulb horn. The engine had neither dipstick nor oil gauge but I knew that it required a pint of oil every fifty miles, and I therefore carried several bottles of oil in a special little box on the stepboard. It was a very reliable vehicle and was never on the end of a towrope, but it had to be driven carefully as it had a metal-to-metal cone clutch which was very fierce, as well as pretty poor brakes. We had some marvellous holidays with it, in spite of the fact that sometimes it had to have a helping push up hills and in holding it back downhill when off the beaten track. After a few years, we gave it to our farmer friend, who took the body off and put it in the farmyard where he used it to sleep in when the farm was overcrowded.

Left: *Me in my fireman's uniform. I was a part-time, voluntary fireman with the N.F.S. from 1938 until 1942.*

Bottom left: *An early recovery crane made by Mannings.*

Bottom right: *Myself standing by one of the planes I flew in my 74th year.*

The Manning grandchildren. Among these there are now a vet, garden-centre manager, pilot, beautician, manageress, joiner (Australia), a secretary, and two of them have degrees.

Percy Manning's 'Little Giant'. One-quarter scale models of a 1904 Charles Burrell traction engine and a fairground organ built by myself in Southport and donated to the Chester Friends of the Imperial Cancer Research Fund.

A Leyland 32-seater coach built by Mannings in the 1920s.

Ford 7-ton van supplied in the early 1920s.

The first motor horse box made by my father.

This was the first charabanc that we made. It was called a traffic chassis and was very robust. The front end was carried in a semicircle in front of the radiator which made it a bit awkward to get at the starting handle. The chassis came from America and was left-hand drive, so I had to convert it to right-hand to comply with police regulations. It had solid tyres for the first season (1922) but later on Goodrich developed giant pneumatic tyres and I converted the hubs to take them. Rated at two-ton capacity, the springs were a bit stiff for passenger carrying, but nobody seemed to notice. Cast aluminium headlamps were available, but we kept the paraffin side- and tail-lamps as stand-bys. It had a whistle on one of the cylinders which was operated by a cord to the steering column. If a sudden shower came on everybody got wet before the hood was put up, and sometimes the lamps would blow out. I hated driving these machines and I was very glad when we got so busy, both running and building a fleet, that I had to spend the rest of my time in the works, except when I used to collect new chassis, or two home a breakdown.

This was the first purpose-made passenger carrying chassis, imported from America in 1925. It was called a Reo Pullman. It was also the first to use four-wheel brakes, self-starters, windscreen wipers and a heating system taken off the exhaust pipe. Walter Manning designed and made what, at the time, was very elegant bodywork. This photograph shows the all-weather equipment (which again my father introduced) which consisted of celluloid screens across each row of seats and along both sides, and knee rugs were provided to all seats. These coaches could do up to 60 miles per hour and were economical in use, although the engines had to be de-carbonised every 8,000 miles, otherwise the exhaust valves used to burn out.

This was the first attempt to make a Sunshine Coach and was called a safety coach, as the windows were wooden-framed and covered in celluloid, which was later changed to glass because the celluloid discoloured. Later on, sliding roofs were developed, although they didn't admit as much sunshine as this first model.

The first buses had a door that opened outwards, which was both dangerous and inconvenient. Eventually, a door was designed in two halves, and to open inwardly. It was operated by the driver reaching across and pulling a handle, hence its name 'the one-man operated door'. But on a wide bus the driver would have to leave his seat to reach the handle, so I designed and made a device to operate the door using suction from the engine, which was very satisfactory. As we were very busy, I contacted several firms who made coach fittings, but could not get them interested in manufacturing the parts – the general belief being that the authorities would not agree to a mechanically operated door. It wasn't long, however, before they were operating on trains as well as buses, but I had let my patent rights lapse so I ended up in debt rather than a rich man.

Right: *One of the first vehicles to be fitted with the newly developed rubber clencher tyres. These were a great improvement in easy riding, quietness and wheel life on the old rough, sett roads. This cart was called a shandry and was used for delivery.*

Centre: *An early Daimler coach.*

Bottom: *A powerful Lancia coach.*

Another vehicle built by Mannings – a Reo Pullman with the distinctive logo of the Manning firm on the elegant coachwork.

Rather a crowded coach party, but happy nevertheless.

A Cugnot steam tractor, 1770, in the Science Museum, London.

A lady's boneshaker of around 1870.

A Doubleday and Humber tricycle from 1878.

Juvenile ordinary bicycle from 1880.

Double perambulator from the mid-nineteenth century.

Perambulator, 1876.

A Benz motor tricycle, 1885.

Lawson's Bicyclette, 1879.

A Rudge rotary tricycle, 1880.

Daimler motorcycle from 1885.

Believe it or not, a Hildebrand prototype steam(!) motorcycle of 1889.

Horse-drawn charabanc, 1890.

A Liverpool horse tram of 1890.

Rudge ordinary penny-farthing bicycle with pneumatic tyres, from 1892.

A Raleigh tandem cycle from 1897.

A Bersey electric cab, 1897.

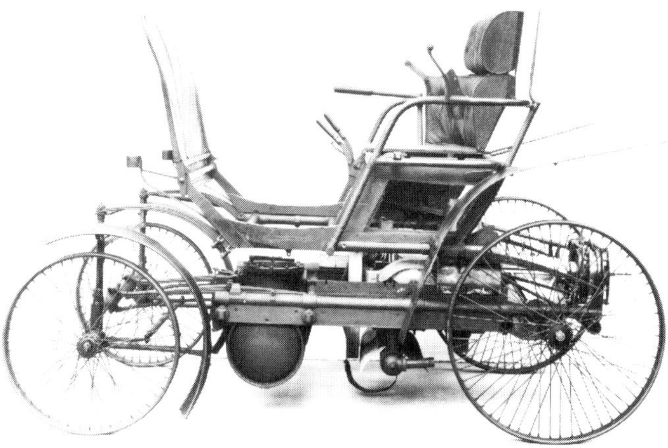

A Lanchester 8-horsepower, 1897.

An Ariel 2¾-horsepower motor tricycle of 1898.

A De Dion Bouton tricycle, 1898.

An 8-horsepower Peugeot car of 1902. We had a car very similar to this called a Briton, I think, and my father and I used it quite a lot jogging around the country on business.

A Humberette motor car, 1903.

White steam car, 1903. Just fancy, we took one of these models in part-exchange for one of the new Ford Toners. I smashed it up for scrap! What a beautiful double-acting cylinder engine it had!

A Wolseley 7½-horsepower car of 1903. We had a Wolseley slightly later than this and it had the engine on its side, crossways in the chassis frame.

A Ford Model-N of 1906. Note the Stepney wheels which clipped on to the road wheels in the event of a puncture. Most early cars had these and when they were fitted they made steering a bit difficult.

Standard coal delivery wagon with compulsory weighing scales.

Rolls Royce 40- to 50-horsepower Silver Ghost of 1909.

A Foden steam wagon, 1910. It was a cold, miserable job for the steersman, who sat on the outside.

An L.G.O.C. B-type motor omnibus of 1910. We had some of these in the army that had been taken over to carry the troops.

A Lanchester 38-horsepower, 1912. Some models had tiller steering!

A chain gearbox for a motor bus, c.1910. This was called a constant-mesh gearbox. Various gear changes were effected by sliding dogs, which was very reliable – gear wheels in those days didn't last long with rough handling.

A Triumph 3½-horsepower, 1911. Note the pedals which were used to start the machine. You could remove the spark plug and use the bike manually, leaving the option of pedalling home!

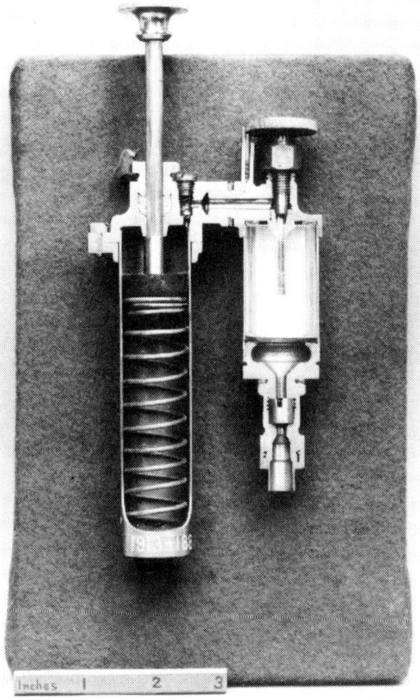

Best and Lloyd drip-feed lubricator for motor cycles, 1913. Most bikes had one of these fitted in the oil tank, at the front of the petrol tank. During normal operation you would press it down every five miles.

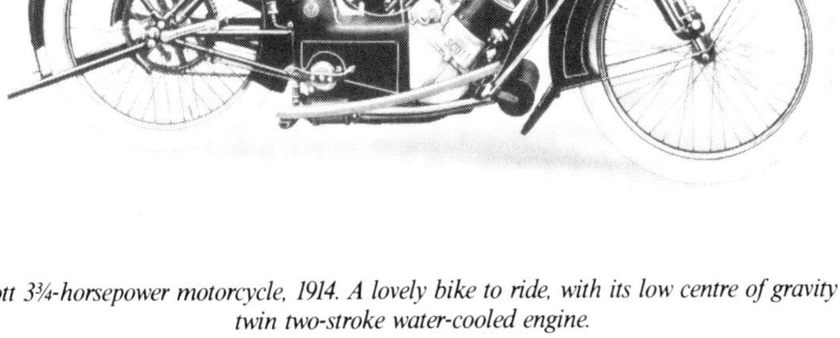

A Scott 3¾-horsepower motorcycle, 1914. A lovely bike to ride, with its low centre of gravity and twin two-stroke water-cooled engine.

A Morgan cycle car of 1913.

A Douglas 2¾-horsepower of 1914. A lovely little bike to ride, with its horizontally opposed engine. You could sit on it and paddle it off to a start, hot or cold, but you had to watch your clothes didn't get caught in the outside flywheel!

Triumph H of 1917. I think this was the first chain-cum-belt model and I rode one quite a lot in the army.

An ABC 3-horsepower of 1919.

A Wallasey motor bus from 1920. This looks like one of the lorry chassis that we had in the army which were fitted with 45-horsepower engines (the one that developed camshaft trouble, as I described in the text). Note the overhanging back axle – one can't help wondering how it never tipped up!

A Zenith Gradua, 6-horsepower, 1920. I had one very similar to this, only much earlier, about 1914, and it was my pride and joy. I rode many thousands of trouble-free miles with only the occasional belt breakage.

A 6-ton Sentinel steam wagon from 1920. Some models had steam-operated tipping gear.

A Shell Dennis petrol wagon – one of the first typical half-cabs that gave a bit of protection against the weather.

A Royal Enfield 8-horsepower of 1921 – a very powerful combination.

An Austin 7 prototype,. 748cc, 1922.

A Triumph 2½-horsepower from 1924.

A Bentley sports car, 1924.

Harley Davidson 7/9-horsepower, 1925. this had a very low riding position, which was infinitely preferable to, for example, some 9-horsepower Indians we had in 1917 from the Canadian Forestry Corps which were very difficult to ride – even the tallest man couldn't reach the floor!

A Ner-a-car, 2¾-horsepower motorcycle, 1925.

Ford Model-T chassis, 1925. I think that this model had been in production since 1911. There is not much of it; that's why people called it the 'flying bedstead! But it was very reliable and Henry Ford certainly laughed all the way to the bank.

Scammell 100-ton lorry, 1929. The rear end was controllable and had a second driver seated on it!

Pressed steel body, 1931, of an Austin 12-6. It was one of the first mass-produced car bodies.

The Lucas dip-and-switch headlamps from 1931. I myself took out a patent for the idea before this but could not get any manufacturer to make it, so I destroyed my patent.

A Cyclemaster motor wheel, 1952.

Right: *A delivery tricycle box lyte, 1938. Note Walls' invitation to 'Stop me and buy one'. Many people will remember this lovely vehicle being pedalled, around the streets.*

Below: *A Raleigh Chopper bicycle from the 1970s. Many of the old cars and bikes look very strange to us now but, who knows, in fifty years or so, this bike may be the cause of many a chuckle. Even now it looks dated and a little bizarre.*

breakdown truck and would set off for home the following morning. This was all very tiring as I had been working all day in the works and I would arrive home absolutely tired out.

Because we were very fond of camping out one of the first things my father made was a motor caravan which I have already described. My mother was always inviting friends to come with us on outings and one day she invited one of the girls from the pictures to come with us to Parbold. We were walking up the hill and we decided to sit down on the bank somewhere and eventually she started to tell me about her underclothes. I naturally thought that this was an invitation, but when I started to have a look she gave me such a clout across the ear, and that put an end to that little episode. A few months later, however, she had a baby but I don't think for one moment if anything had happened between us on that day she would have blamed me. Nevertheless it is something which rather upset my calculations at the time.

We had fast motorbikes in those days and I had, at that time, a 6-horse Zenith with a graduate gear. This graduate gear consisted of you turning a handle on the tank, the pulley wheel expanded at the same time as the back wheel was moved backwards so that the tension on the belt was always kept the same. This was an admirable way of gearing because you could suit the gear to whatever incline you were going up. The only trouble was that they were pretty heavy on the belts. When the Zeniths were entered in various hill climbing competitions they invariably won because, as I have said, you could adjust the gear to the engine speed and conditions. Eventually, however, they would not have them in the speed trials and hill climbing events because they always won. My particular bike had lapped Brooklands at 84 m.p.h. in 1912 which was a terrific speed in those days. Eventually, I made a side car for it. I bought the chassis and made a hexagonal shape and every dimension was 24 inches. I then took it out to test it and found that there was such a big rake on the forks that I had a terrific effort to steer it round corners. I was very disappointed, but it just wasn't suitable. It was about this time I decided to get married and I thought that as I used to go so fast on it I had better get rid of it before I had an accident.

At this time I heard about a firm in Preston who made a cycle car called an ML and it had a Jap 10 h.p. vertical twin water-cooled engine. There were a few completed vehicles, and also quite a lot of parts and we bought the whole lot for quite a reasonable price. We sold a completed one and then I built up the others from the spare parts.

One day I went to Liverpool with my father on business and he decided to call in and see an old family friend from the days when he lived in Bootle. He hadn't seen them for quite a while and they kindly invited us to stay for tea. They had quite a big family – nine brothers and sisters. I fell for the eldest sister right away and my father invited them to come to Wales with us to the caravan. They lived in a big house in Bootle called 'Manor House.' Her mother had died recently and her father had employed a housekeeper. Whilst we were away in Wales, her father decided to marry the housekeeper. He had told the children that when they returned from Wales they would have a new mother. Of course, they were all terribly upset. I'll never forget it.

However, I was more or less in charge of the family and we had to sleep in one big tent. The children really enjoyed themselves and I had to go home and leave them and then go back and pick them up again after a few days. We became very friendly and I was often invited to the house for the weekend. I would stay over the weekend and during the week I used to go on the train on a Wednesday night and I invariably took so long saying goodnight that I would have to do the final gallop when I heard the last train coming in the distance. I would end up at the station badly out of breath. One night I missed the train but there was always a baggage car which came along a few minutes later. However, it was not supposed to take passengers, but I knew the driver, so he would invite me into the cab.

After her mother's death my lady friend became very depressed, and although her father and stepmother were very good in some respects, he expected the children to do as he wished. One night he asked my future wife to dress up her stepmother in her late mother's jewellery. This upset her terribly. It was making her ill living under these conditions, especially as she had lost a mother whom she had adored. I could see that she was becoming very thin, and I said to her, 'Well, you stick it out as long as you can, and when you can't stick it any longer, I'll find a way out of it.' Eventually, we went to see one of her late mother's friends and asked her what she thought the solution could be. She said, 'Well, if you love one another, why don't you get married?' I put this suggestion to my young lady and she was all for it. Unfortunately, she was not of age, but I knew a registrar very well and he told me that we would either have to go and live in Scotland for three weeks or else we would have to declare a false age. Really he should not have told me this. We were very busy at the time and it was impossible for us to go and live in Scotland for three weeks. I went to see my solicitor and told him that we were thinking of getting married and told him that we would have to declare a false age and asked him what would happen if the law found out. He looked it up and said, 'A fine not exceeding £100.00 or 12 months in jail.' So he said 'Are you going to do it?' 'Yes,' I said, 'I am.'

On the eve of our elopement a very sad thing happened. My elder brother had a lovely little girl who was nine months old and she had some complaint which the doctors could not diagnose. Sadly she died so we got the family together and asked them what we should do. They said that the only thing we could do was to go ahead, for if we postponed it we may never get another chance to elope. As you can well imagine, I was very reluctant to do this, but on the other hand, it was the only thing we could do at the time. We made all the arrangements to elope and I went with a Model T Ford on Good Friday to pick her up. The night before, she had managed to smuggle out some clothes in a case which she had left at the home of her late mother's friend. I met her there and came to Southport. I had this special licence and we went to a church to get married. During the ceremony the church door banged and I looked round quickly expecting to see her father. We went on our honeymoon the same day down to the gamekeepers cottage in Market Drayton. My mother and father were all in favour of our marriage.

When we arrived at Warrington I thought it best that we send a telegram to her father so that he would not be worried too much. The only place I was able to send one from was a Police Station, and so I went in and saw the policeman on duty. I asked him if he could send a telegram, and he asked me if it was urgent as they were not supposed to. When I told him what it was and that we had just eloped and we wanted to send a telegram to her father, he laughed and said, 'O.K.' I gave him half a crown and I worded the telegram: 'Just married, off on honeymoon.' It was to be the start of 60 happy years and to this day I have never regretted the fact that we eloped.

When we got back from our honeymoon, we wrote to her father explaining what had happened and enquiring as to whether we would be welcome to come back home again. Sadly, he never replied and he completely cut us off which was a great shame because he missed out on a lot of pleasures. He never even saw his grandchildren and, regrettably, the only time my wife saw her father was when she went to visit him in hospital when he was dying.

On the anniversary of our first honeymoon we decided to have a holiday at the same gamekeeper's cottage, and we went yet again in the same old Model T. Ford. I was out one day with Joe, the gamekeeper, and we came across some ladies' footprints. We were right out in the wilds and Joe just could not understand this. So he thought that we had better get back home, and as soon as we came within sight of the cottage they were waving frantically for us to come. It appeared that my wife, who was 7-months pregnant, was very ill and they thought that she was going to have a miscarriage. In the meantime, whilst we were away, the lady we were staying with went out on her bicycle to find the midwife. They came to see to my wife, but apparently, it was very troublesome as the baby was breached. My wife was having a very rough time, so they told me that I must go and find a doctor as quickly as possible. It was three miles back to the town and I rushed round all the narrow country lanes. I tried three different doctors, and I am quite sure that one of them was at home, because I heard the maid more or less telling the doctor that we needed help, but with us being strangers they were reluctant to come out. Eventually, I went back to the cottage and the midwife sent a note down to say that I must get a doctor at any price, so I reversed the old Ford, which took quite a while to turn round, and thought to myself 'I'll have that fellow out by the scruff of the neck if I have to.' However, just as soon as I had turned round and was setting off again, they called me back and said that there was no need to hurry now as my wife had given birth and the child was stillborn. I still had to get the doctor, but I went back a little later on and went to one of the doctors, who was an elderly man, and I told him what had happened. He said, 'Righto sonny, I'll come right away.' He came out and saw my wife and informed us what a wonderful job the midwife had done, and that he needn't do anything else.

'How is it, doctor, that this has happened when my wife has taken every possible care of herself, and I have even put new tyres and special springs on the car so that she would not be unduly jolted and at any risk?' I asked.

'Well, lad, it's all part of nature; you think yourself very lucky that you have got your wife, you are only young and there is plenty of time to try again.'

However, my wife looked very ill, and as I had to come home because we were so busy, I left her there for a fortnight. I went back and brought her home and it was seven years before she became pregnant again. It was a very anxious time for me and I will never forget the goodness of the lady of the house. They would not accept any payments whilst we were there, so as they did not have a radio I decided to give them one. I fitted an aerial up on the roof and eventually we were able to get it to work. Joe was highly delighted, and he would sit with the headphones on for hours listening to it.

We were all very sorry when Joe's boss decided that it was becoming too expensive rearing pheasants and gave him notice to quit. Joe moved away to the Midlands and sadly we lost touch with him. Joe's eldest boy had just left school and wanted a job and father invited him over to ask him if he would like to become a bodybuilder. He came to work for us and was very quick to pick things up. I had shown him how to light the blow lamp and one night I wanted him to do a job for me and told him to go and light it. All of a sudden I heard a terrific roar, and when I went to see what was the matter, he had the blowlamp on top of the smithy fire getting it hot. He said that he had put methylated spirits on and had thought that this was a much quicker way of doing it! However, he could not settle down after living in the country and the open life, so he went back to join his family.

Chapter Nine

Liquidation

AFTER the old firm went into liquidation, I went into the sales office of a garage and found the owner. I told him that I had come on what he may think was, perhaps, a funny mission. 'I want to buy that coach you are advertising, but I have no money,' I said. I explained what had happened to our business and he became very interested. He said, 'Well, I think we can perhaps come to some arrangement.' 'Well, what I really want,' I said, 'is for you to let us have this on a hire purchase agreement and licence and insure it for us and then my father will be able to carry straight on working.' 'Fair enough, come back on Monday morning and it will be ready for you,' he said. So I did so, and he let us have the coach without any deposit, just a note to pay him, which, of course, we did. Father was happy because he had something to do, and we found a yard at the back of some shops where they let us garage it.

To bring it up to date, father made some back rests for the seats because they were just the ordinary low back seats. It had a salon body and he laboriously made the back rests and fitted it out and then started work. He was then able to get some of the old drivers to help out part time. Before the old firm went into liquidation, father had made two big furniture vans. We had 18 coaches during the winter and the majority of these were laid up. He had the idea of taking the coach bodies off and putting big pantechnicons on, and he designed them so that there was a double row of seats in the front. There was a seat where the driver and two or three passengers would sit, and immediately behind that was another wide row of seats for other passengers with the furniture. We became very busy and travelled all over the country.

I then had the idea of fixing up father with a furniture van, and I had seen a Reo Pulman advertised in a Wigan paper for £25. My mother had saved up an odd pound or two so I went over and had a look at it and we were able to buy it. It was not in very good condition, however, but for £25 it had a lorry flat on it and a detachable box van which we cut in half to make it wider and mounted it on the lorry body. We then built the front of it over the driver's seat at the front of the radiator, which gave a lot more room up above. In fact, he was able to carry two or three piece suites in the fore peak.

I knew people at the Marine Stores who had bought all the scrap from our place, including all sorts of new crown wheels, pinions, pistons, con rods and all sorts of things. They let me have the whole lot for £2. Whilst father was altering the body, I took the engine out and thoroughly overhauled it. It was just around Christmas time when we managed to get it roadworthy and we licensed and insured it.

The post office were advertising for vehicles to deliver post over the Christmas period, so I applied. It was for 10 days at 30/- a day, which to us was a fortune. I drove the van and father would get up very early with me each morning to help start it up. It was difficult to start as there was no self starter and someone had to be on the carburettor whilst the other was on the handle.

With the money we made we were able to buy some second-hand tyres which were of various sizes and the van looked very peculiar from behind because it had a big tyre on the outside at the back, and on the inside was a much smaller one. I did manage to get two fairly respectable ones on the front and they lasted us quite a long time before we were able to buy new ones.

Father was developing rheumatism in his wrists and it was sad to see him struggling with the furniture. For instance, if we were loading a piano, I used to lift the piano up at one end and give it to him and he sort of rested it on his arms and then I would pick it up at the other end.

We were due to take quite a big load down to London and we started to load up at 8 a.m. on the Thursday morning. Father and I set off at lunchtime on the Thursday. We only had enough money to buy the petrol to get us there, so instead of putting up for the night, and as I didn't feel too tired we carried on through the night.

We arrived at Seven Oaks at 10 a.m. on the Friday morning. The house was over the shop so we had to hoist everything up from the outside and through the windows, so by this time, I was feeling tired. We managed to unload, and then the lady fixed us up with a good feed of ham and eggs. We were paid £10, which again was a small fortune, and we were then able to fill up with petrol and start back for home on the Friday afternoon.

We arrived back in Liverpool at midnight and we were to have loaded up again for another journey. However, we knocked the chap up and by this time I was very weary. He was very irate because we should have been there earlier in the day and he fell out with us and told us that he did not require our services. I was glad, but father was disappointed because of the money. We arrived home in the early hours of Saturday morning and I was that tired and weary that I had a job to find my way home after I had garaged the van, as I had been on the road from 8 a.m. on the Thursday.

Another unfortunate experience my father had was when he was taking a load of furniture to Windermere. He came to a notorious hill and it was a very long pull up, and the driver was not very competent, although he had been at the job for years. He was in bottom gear and was having great difficulty in climbing up the remainder of the hill, so he slipped the clutch and, of course, the clutch eventually burnt out. He had to let it run back on some waste land and then he managed to get someone to come and have a look at it. They informed him that it would have to have new plates. If I had been there at the time I would have got out my spanner and slackened a couple of muts off on the cross shaft and readjusted the clutch pedal. Instead of doing that they charged him a terrific amount for replacing the clutch plates. Of course, he spent more on the repairs than he received for the job.

In the early part of the 1920s we bought vehicles from America which apparently had been ex-workers' cars. They used them for 12 months and then traded them in so they were all mostly in good condition. I remember one called an Overland which was a 10 h.p. open tourer. We used it for a little while for ourselves and I went out in it one night without telling my father, and I took three or four of the girls from the picture palace. We went for a ride and it was a lovely moonlit night but unfortunately, I had forgotten to switch the headlights on. Eventually, a policeman pulled us up but fortunately he let me off. He did not book me which was a good job becuse I would have got into very serious trouble with my father.

There was an electrician from Windermere who had bought a Fiat open coach from us and I went to deliver it, and also to teach him to drive. He said to me when I first arrived, 'Oh, I'll soon pick it up, I know all about it.' However, he did not, and I was three days with him. Each time his wife came with us and she said to me one day, 'I wish he would hurry up and learn to drive because I'm going to keep coming with him whilst he is driving; if he is going to get killed, I want to be killed with him.' I thought that wasn't very cheerful.

Another thing happened to a Fiat in Bowness. It was an open Fiat lorry with sideboards on, and a very nice chap had bought it who worked at the railway station. He would deliver anything for anyone who came by train. He also developed a furnishing removal business and I drove to Bowness and taught him to drive, which he picked up quite quickly.

One day a chap came into the works on a bicycle and wanted to order a two and a half tonne Fiat, which he did, and then he went pedalling back on his bike some 60-odd miles. When the wagon was ready, he came down on his bike again and settled up. He then put his bike on the wagon and we set off. I drove it out of Southport and then I let him have a go. He had never driven before in his life, but he drove it to the outskirts of Preston and then I took over and drove through Preston, then he took over and drove it all the way to his home to a place called Hawes. It was in a very hilly part and when he got to his home he switched off and said, 'Well, we'll have to take this wall down now.' We had to set to, there and then and take down a stone wall so we could get the lorry into the shed. He was a tough country man and I said to him, 'Well, where shall we go tomorrow?' 'Oh, you're going home today,' he replied. 'Well,' I said, 'you won't be able to manage.' 'Oh,' he said, 'I'll manage alright. Now you get off home and thank you very much.' So I did and we never heard any more from him.

Then we started building buses with driver operated doors. The doors were in two parts and there was an extension handle with which the driver, by reaching over, could hold and open the door without having to leave his seat. I got the idea of making them work by compressed air, and developed a cylinder which worked from suction from the inlet pipe from the engine, and it opened and closed the doors very effectively. I tried to manufacture this, but I could not get anyone interested in doing it. I was told that the authorities would not give permission to use doors which opened mechanically. Of course, this proved to be entirely wrong, as very soon after, railway trains were using self operating doors. This was a great disappointment to me.

When I was driving a coach there were no such things as dipping headlights. When you met someone on the road it was one big glare. At the time there was a Barkers Dipping Headlamp already on the market, but these were only fitted to Rolls Royce and Morris Oxford cars. It was a cluttered, mechanical affair, worked by a lever from the driver's seat, and the headlamps were on heavy brackets. I was looking at these one day and I thought to myself that it was only the reflector that needed to be dipped. So, I set to and made a dipping reflector which worked off the induction by suction and I also made it so that it would work from the battery. The drivers at Blackpool just could not believe that I had invented this. I tried to get it manufactured and I was introduced to a gentleman who had money. He was a great financial wizard and he used to invest in various things. I told him what I wanted and he seemed very impressed. I said that I intended making, say two or three hundred sets and selling them, and then perhaps would make another two or three humdred and sell those too. He said unfortunately he wasn't interested and that if I had asked him for £10,000, he most probably would have been more interested, so I got nothing. I wrote to several Companies, including Lucas, to enquire if they would market it. They informed me that there already was a dipping headlamp on the market. It seems that they waited until my patent had expired and I had thrown out all the papers connected with the patent. One day I was sitting in the dentist's looking at some motoring magazines, and discovered that Lucas were marketing a dipping reflector and selling millions of sets. Every car was being fitted with a Lucas dipping reflector. I was talking to my bank manager soon after this. I used to look after his Daimler car for him, and I told him what had happened. 'Go and get me the papers' he said. I told him that I had been so upset about the whole business that I had burnt everything connected with it. 'What a pity, but they can't get away with a thing like that,' he said. I told him that I understood that there were people who go searching the patent offices looking for something they could eventually steal. If only I had kept those papers, he could have done something about it for me, and if I had only received say, sixpence royalty on each set I would have been a millionaire.

Whilst I was in the army I sent up an idea for the searchlights to be interconnected with the anti-aircraft guns. Although they were able to pick out the aircraft with a searchlight, they were unable to get the range and correct sighting with the guns. I could not see why they did not put the two together, so that when the searchlights were on it, they would at least be in sight. They said that it would not operate, but I understand later, that it was in fact used.

The army lorry park had quite a big incline, which was handy on cold mornings when the engines were difficult to start. We were able to park quite a few at the top of this hill, and in the morning set off down, letting the clutch in, and thereby starting the engine. One day I was coming down fairly fast with my FWD wagon, when all of a sudden I saw the sergeant major carrying a stick. I nearly knocked him down and, of course, I was severely reprimanded for going so fast.

We also kept wagons at a German prisoner-of-war camp, and one day I was there and the Germans were singing the German Hymn of Hate. I don't know why they called it that, or what the actual words meant, but it meant something to do with hating the English. We had a big press there which was used for pressing on solid tyres. It had to be pumped up to 100 tons pressure by turning a big wheel. I used to get the Germans to turn the wheel to get the pressure up and sometimes when the tyre wasn't on properly we had to press it off again to put it back on to the wheel.

One day it was raining quite hard and some of the wagons were fitted with a cheap American magneto called a Dixie Mag. This was alright if it was dry, but when it was raining it would short out. I was trying to get one of these wagons going and I had two of the Germans on the handle, and they pretended not to know how to put the handle in to turn it. They also pretended not to know any English. However, you should have heard them after they had been turning the engine for a while, they certainly knew how to curse in English.

The officers' cars were 20 horse power Daimlers with a square type saloon body. It was one of the first type of saloons made, but it had one fault. The gearbox was on the back axle, which meant that there was a lot of unsprung weight, so unfortunately we had a lot of back axle trouble with them. Apart from this, the engine was very reliable indeed.

We had a batch of 20 horse power Vauxhall open 5-seater tourers delivered, and they had 4 cylinder engines on them which were very solid. I think they had an extra main bearing because they had such a lovely beat with the exhaust. One of the Vauxhalls belonged to a big red-faced Colonel who had a chest full of ribbons. He wanted a self-starter fixed on this car, so the O.C. gave me the job to do. I just don't remember where we got the tooth ring which had to be shrunk onto the flywheel. Of course, they were open flywheels, there was no covering as they had a separate gearbox. I fitted these rings quite successfully on the flywheel and put it all back again, and then I had the job of making brackets to fit the starter motor on to. When eventually I had finished the job and tried it out, it seemed to be quite satisfactory. When the Colonel came, he was a rough type of chap. I hoped everything would be satisfactory which, in the event, it was. He got into the seat and pressed the button and was highly delighted with it. He complimented me on having done such a good job. That was a really nice model and very reliable. I will always remember the hefty beat that it had on its exhaust.

We also had several 10-horsepower Singer open two seaters which also had the gearbox on the back axle, and the lady drivers would drive these. We used to get quite a bit of trouble with the back axle because there was so much unsprung weight. My favourite ride throughout my army career was the 4-horse Douglas. It was a lovely bike fitted with a three speed gearbox, a clutch and kick start and it had a lovely beat with its exhaust due to the cylinders being horizontally opposite. It had a sidecar fitted which was full of tools and spares. When eventually I went to get demobbed, I went to Crewe and along with several others, arrived fairly late in the day and had to queue. N.C.O.s and Privates were carrying our personal belongings. There was a male Lance Corporal bossing us around which, of course, he knew very well he could do because we were being demobbed. It took some time for us to get our papers cleared. We were allowed to keep our greatcoats and we were issued with a civilian suit. By this time it was very late and we had to stay at Preeze Heath which was quite a few miles from Crewe. It was a very muddy and dirty place and we were issued with some filthy blankets and shown into a hut and given some very crude tea. However, three or four of us lived in the Lancashire area and we got together and decided to try and get a taxi to Crewe. We were quite sure that we would get a connection to Liverpool, which we eventually did. We got a taxi and duly arrived in Crewe. I then caught a connection to Liverpool and the other lads caught their connections to Manchester, and so it all ended happily.

Chapter Ten

Turbulent Times Ahead

WHEN the old firm W. Manning went into liquidation, my wife and I lived at home at Kew Road with my parents. We lived with them for three years until we had sufficient money to get a place of our own. We managed to get a brand new house in Lyndhurst Road, which we rented for £1 a week, and we lived in this for twelve months. During this time I saw an empty shop and house down one of the main roads and I had the idea of my wife, my younger brother who was an electrician, and myself opening an electrical shop in Liverpool Road, which we did eventually. After I had finished at the works, I would work until midnight, with a candle in one hand and a trowel in the other, bricklaying. I made the building into two flats and rewired and ashphalted it. We received rent for the flat which in turn paid for the mortgage.

Eventually, I obtained the Hornby Train Agency. I had always been interested in model railways and for the three weeks prior to Christmas we would have a lay-out in the shop of a model railway. It was surprising how many people would come into the shop after Christmas with a broken engine or something and they would ask if we could repair it for them. I would ask them if they had bought it from us, but they nearly always said that they had bought it from Lewis's in Liverpool and they did not want the bother of having to take it back there. They would rather pay to have it repaired.

We also obtained an HMV Agency and I made an audition room at the rear of the shop where there had been an old shed. I did not obtain planning permission and one Christmas eve I received a letter from the Corporation to say that one of their inspectors had seen the building and that if we did not take it down within two weeks they would come and take it down themselves. So after the Christmas holidays I went to see the planning engineer and told him that I understood that if you used existing footings of a building then you did not need to have plans.

He informed me that this was not so, and that you still needed to have plans to make sure that the right materials were used. We had a felt roof which did not fit in with the surrounding properties. If we agreed to slate the roof we would be given permission. So we did and we were!

My wife and younger brother were now running the business and we had a good collection of wirelesses. We sold many of the original wireless kits which were brought out, and I made one of the very first radiograms which was a four-valve set. I also fitted a record player in it, and it was one of the first commercially built radiogramophones. Incidentally, I also fitted a microphone onto it.

We also had a battery-charging service and I bought a brand new motor generator. At first I used to charge off the lights in the shop as resistance, and one time the assistant manager from the Electricity Board came round and said that he understood from one of his inspectors that we were using the lights in the shop for charging batteries when we should have been paying power price. There were three prices: lighting, power and some other charge. Lighting was one penny a unit and power was twopence halfpenny, but eventually this all had to go.

There was enough room on the shop front for a couple of coaches and from this we received a good revenue. However, again, when the old firm W. Manning went into liquidation, all my money had been tied up in guarantees and I had a great shock when I came to take stock in my own business. In the end I thought that I had about two hundred pounds worth, but I found out that I had nine hundred pounds worth of stock. I had no idea how I was going to pay for it. I borrowed £200 from the bank, but in the end they forclosed on me. I had to sign a Deed of Assignment and the shop was closed. I had to sell up, which was very sad, especially having spent so much time and money on the premises. I had very little left to repay on the mortgage, but when you lose everything and you have no money, especially as we had a young family, you do not stop to think too much. So we went back and lived with my mother. We were so hard up that the only thing that was left to us was the bedding. They took everything including our furniture, apart from the clothes we wore. I remember having to move the bedding by putting it on a pram and taking it my mother's house.

When the time came to move all the stuff from the shop I had made a counter and I remember it cost £1 a foot to buy a counter. I wanted a 12-foot counter so I made one out of battens and covered it with some nice mahogany-coloured plywood. I stained and varnished it and actually it only cost me about fifteen shillings. However, when the removal men came to take all the stuff away they were unable to get the counter out through the door, so instead of leaving it there for perhaps some future buyer, they just smashed it up with an axe in front of my eyes and I could have killed them. They simply piled it into the van as firewood.

Another upsetting feature was when the notice was put up regarding the sale. One of my old schoolmates came and said, 'I'm sorry to hear about your trouble. Is there anything going cheap at the sale?' This was the general attitude.

Next door to the shop lived a professor who had an Austin car which I used to look after. I went round and told him what had happened, and he said, 'Why didn't you tell me, I would have lent you the money to pay off your mortgage.' If I had known, and if I hadn't been so upset at having no money, and just sat it out, as it were, we could have got going again, but, then it was too late. I learned a lesson then that any business in the future that I might enter into would have a complete check on what was going on in the office. This was one of the downfalls of our old company, really, because we had a nice old gentleman who was the secretary and the other directors would just tell him what to do. He must have known what was going on, but he was too conscientious, I suppose, to start telling tales. When eventually I did start up business again I made it my business to keep my eye on everything, including timesheets, and to check all the invoices in an endeavour not to make the same mistakes again.

One Sunday afternoon when it was tippling down with rain we were all sitting in the parlour and we heard somebody singing out in the street. My mother looked through the window and there was a young couple with a baby. They were absolutely soaked. They were singing beggars, but mother invited them in and helped to get them dry and gave them a good hot meal and a little money, which she could ill afford, and sent them on their way.

This was typical of my mother, always ready to help and the same thing applied to my father. I have known him more than once let a tradesman have a new vehicle and he would say, 'Let's help them all we can'. On a Saturday morning it was my job to go around and get various amounts from people who owed us money for the different jobs and I really hated having to approach, say, a big burly butcher and ask him if he could pay something on account. One time we sold a brand new bus for £900. A chap came up from Nottingham and he appeared to be a decent chap. He had no money, however, but he had this opinion that he could get good contracts, taking girls to work.

Father let him have this bus without any deposit. He had to sign the hire purchase papers and each month end accounts were sent out and he never paid. This went on for about eight months and then the hire purchase company, because we were the guarantors, said that we had to go and reclaim the bus.

I was taken to a gypsy camp and our bus was there. I had a good look at it and it looked very rough indeed. I took off my jacket and hung it on some shafts of a cart standing nearby and carried on trying to get the bus started but it was in such a hopeless mess. I did manage to get the tyres blown up and when I came to put my jacket on, my wallet had gone - stolen! So then I had to go back to the police station and ask them if they could lend me enough money to get home. I made arrangements for the bus to be collected, put on the train and brought back to Southport. When we went to look it over in Southport we decided it just wasn't worth repairing so we simply scrapped it. The chap had absolutely run it to death, he had run it for miles and worked it night and day and, no doubt, he made a lot of money. When I told my father about this, he said, 'Oh well, it won't do him any good. There's no use crying over spilt milk, let's get on with it'. So I said to him, 'Well, if you had met this fellow in the army and you realised what some people would do you would possibly have a different attitude'. He never did, and he trusted everybody until he died. He died happy, as did my mother, so I suppose there is something in the saying, 'As you sow, so shall you reap'. You do get a lot of satisfaction out of helping people, even though, of course, a lot will take advantage.

In the early 1920s we were selling quite a lot of Model T Fords and building our own bodies on them. Father made one of the very first milk vans which was an open-sided van and it was quite popular with the milkman.

In those days we usually made sure that we had enough petrol on a journey because the garages were so very few and far between. We had to buy Fords through different Ford agents who were glad to sell them to get rid of their quota and we always got the full discount and sometimes a little bit more. Eventually my father applied for the Ford agency for the Southport area and everything seemed to be going smoothly. Father made arrangements to buy a place in town where we wished to build a garage and showrooms and we had a very go ahead salesman. I bought the Fords and we had to obliterate the engine number so that they could not be traced otherwise the agents would have got into serious trouble. However, when it came to signing the papers to take on the agency, they told father that they expected him to give up all the other vehicles we were selling. We were selling Leylands, Mawdesleys and Dennises, different chassis and putting bodies on them. Father, being a self-made man, wasn't to be dictated to, so he told them that we would not bother with the agency and that we would carry on the way we were. It so happened that the very next year we sold more Fords than the local Ford agent. The salesman was on to a good thing, he was getting 50% profit on the chassis which were sold. The salesman tried all ways to get a sale, but my father, who was always straight forward, had to dismiss him in the end and he started up on his own just around the corner. He started building bodies and he managed to take one or two of our men from us by promising them all sorts of things and then he would go around showing photographs of vehicles we had sold and he led people to believe that he had made them. In the end father had to bring a court case against him to stop him using this information. The unfortunate thing was that a lady friend of ours in Manchester used to buy a Ford chassis on our account and one time father let her have a cheque for £1,000 to go and buy. I suppose it was for two or three chassis but she put this to her own use. We had to have a court case over this because eventually the lady accused my brother of having taken the money, so we had to go to quite a big expense to clear my brother's name which they eventually did but it was a very sad affair.

In 1924 I saw, in one of the motor magazines, an American vehicle called a Reo Pulman which was a very low, six cylinder, fast, passenger chassis built especially for passenger work and apparently it had been used in the States for quite a while where it had proved to be very successful. Therefore, we made arrangements to sell some of these vehicles as we could see the potential. Father designed a nicely-shaped open coach body with an ordinary hood; there was only one step and you were inside as opposed to the old coaches which had three to four steps. It was a very reliable, fast-moving coach and father developed long-distance tours and I am quite sure we were the first to run long distance tours as we now know them. We ran a daily service to Torquay, Bournemouth and Scarborough and also a daily service to Glasgow. These tours proved very popular until around the 1926 period when we took quite a lot of vehicles in part exchange. Of course, they were nearly all solid-tyred vehicles and because the Michelin Tyre Company had brought out giant pneumatic tyres people were very reluctant to ride in a solid-tyred vehicle. We had some in our fleet and it became increasingly difficult to find passengers for them.

In some cases I was able to fit pneumatic tyres by putting new hubs and wheels on if the vehicle was in good condition, but we were left with a lot of vehicles on our hands which severely interrupted our cash flow. When we approached the bank they suggested that we float our company in order to get some extra capital. So they introduced us to three different people who put a nominal amount in. I think it was about £500 each and they were appointed directors of our company. They did not spend a lot of time with us preferring to go playing golf. One was an ex- sea captain and the others had a business arranging holidays. What they would do was hire out coaches and use them in their other business of long-distance tours and we found out that they were paying us £10 per week for a coach and driver and they were making as much as £100 per week in their business.

Whilst on this subject, when we were having a petrol tank installed in our garage the petrol supply went from 2 gallon tins into 40 gallon steel barrels. A firm brought out a device on wheels which held one of these barrels and it also had a pump on it, so that you could put a barrel on, put the pump in and fill up the tanks. Of course, when we had a fleet of coaches it soon emptied the barrel and it was a heavy job putting another full barrel on. We applied for a petrol tank installation and it was called a red line at that time. I was using this red line because I found out that the petrol was very clean and some of the other brands of petrol contained sediments and water but the red line was always nice and clean and it suited our engines. We were able to get the red line people to install a 500 gallon tank so they said that if we dug a hole they would supply the tank and the pump. So we duly dug the hole but we were situated on a part of Southport which they called the ream where the tide level is very near the surface. If you dug a hole just over two feet deep you would come to water. The hole we required had to be about eight feet deep, so we had to put shuttering all around and hired a pump from the Corporation and pumped the water by hand. They delivered the tank but by this time the hole was nearly full of water again, so we put in the tank and got in touch with the petrol people to come and fill the tank. They said, 'Well are you ready for it yet, you haven't concreted round it have you?' 'No', I said, 'we wanted to sink it down in the hole'. 'What do you mean?' I told him that he had better come and have a look, so he came and when he saw the tank floating in the water he exclaimed, 'Oh, my goodness, we can't have that, we can't have a tank floating about in the water'. Father then explained that once it was filled with the petrol it would sink and we would then pump out the water and put in the necessary concrete so that the water would eventually disperse when it was filled with sand.

As I have said before, when the old firm went into liquidation, we had to go and live with my parents. My mother was a good old sort and she was a very good manager. My father grew all the vegetables on his two allotments. In fact he grew so many that he was able to sell some of the vegetables. My mother would buy a sheep's head for sixpence and make some wonderful gravy and broth. We had potatoes, carrots and cabbage which father had grown on his allotment and we managed quite well because it wasn't costing us too much to live. However, father and I were more or less living from day to day on what we could earn and in some cases I was doing odd jobs. Sometimes when we did furniture removal the people would have some odd jobs which they wanted doing and I remember one particular case in which a lady in a rather good neighbourhood, who was a widow with a daughter, asked me to do some alterations inside the house and to tidy her garden.

Father and I decided to try to get a job. Father obtained a job immediately as a joiner just four or five miles away where they were making a new army camp at Freshfield.

He came home one day and told me that the foreman had complimented him on his work and said that he was about the only one who could get to work by 7.30 am. He had to cycle the journey and there were chaps who lived on the doorstep almost who could not get into work on time. However, he thoroughly enjoyed doing this joinery until one day he asked the foreman for a job and the foreman said, 'Oh, go and lose yourself for a few hours Walter, there's nothing much to do'. So the other chaps would play cards, but father couldn't stomach sitting down and playing cards and getting paid for it.

Things were bad in the 1930s and I went to see our old salesman who had started up on his own and who appeared to be doing fairly well. I asked him if he would give me a job and, of course, he was only too pleased because he knew my capabilities. At the time a mechanic's wage was one and twopence-halfpenny an hour. Apparently sheet metal workers' wages were half a crown an hour. I did some electrical and mechanical work and sometimes I would do some blacksmithing. The salesman came to me one day and said that he wanted me to do some panel beating as he was very short, so I didn't object because, after all, it was work. However, his secretary came to me on the Friday and said that the union were kicking up a fuss about me doing this work and they said that they would not have to call me a panel beater, but they didn't mind calling me a sheet metal worker. I didn't mind what they called me so long as I got my money on a Friday night.

The salesman decided to go into ready-made joinery, so he eventually acquired some more machinery. One item was called a four cutter which would do four operations simultaneously and made ready made windows and doors. Then, of course, they had to be delivered so he bought a big Bedford van and I used to drive it and deliver the windows and doors.

In the meantime the salesman decided to sell the van. A gentleman from South Africa came and bought it and we started working as usual. We were making a big furniture van and I was making some iron work for it when this gentleman came up to me and said, 'How long will it be before it is finished?' I told him what I thought and he said, 'Oh, you've taken a long time over it'. So I said, 'I don't think so, I'm just working like I've always worked'. He informed me that he had been looking at the figures from a previous van exactly like this and it had been done in half the time, so we looked into it and found out that the figures had been altered. He was so disgusted by this that eventually he sold out and there again, of course, I was out of work.

I started hunting for another job and one day I heard that Woodwards had an opening. An Altcar firm were the Leyland agents and had a good reputation – we had previously had dealings with this particular firm in 1921. I popped on my bike to the interview. We sold an American wagon called a Kelly Springfield and this firm had just started up as haulage contractors and, of course, they knew what experience I had had and they immediately started me as a general worker. I could do every possible job and the first job I was given was on a Leyland cub. They were body builders and they built a new body on this Leyland cub. I got on very well there. There was one chap there called Teddy. We used to do all the maintenance work on the machinery and the petrol pumps and we also did all the electrical repairs to the self starters and the dynamos. I also did the replating of the batteries and we would do all the welding and cutting. There were things I could do that Teddy couldn't and he could do things that I couldn't but we got on very well and during the four years we worked together we never had a wrong word. Another character at Woodward's was a short-tempered sprayer called Bill Roberts. I also worked for Splicer's in Shakespeare Street, when Walter Jesson (the local historian) was a storeman. Later I went to Kirby's tool room where I remember a chap called Barton who was the bodyworker.

Woodward's manager came to me one time and said that there was rather a lot of body work required on a vehicle. He told me that they could get a mechanic or an electrician to do the work but they could not get a body builder. I told him that I did not mind and that I would be quite happy to do it. They got an electrician who was of the modern type and when it came to a rewiring job he would simply snip off all the wires, make up a new loom and then connect it up. He always wanted one of the mechanics to be with him when he was doing the connecting because he had to sort out all the wires and somebody would have to be at each end. Teddy and I did not crack on to knowing all that much about wiring looms, so we would put little labels on the wires or little dots or paint so that we would recognise them. On the big Leylands the dashboards were made out of some kind of metal which, if they got too hot, would catch fire. The manager asked me about welding these cracks and I told him that it wasn't feasible because of the burning. He asked me what I could suggest so I told him that we could make some brackets and put plenty of quarter bolts in and fix them. We did this and it was quite a success. We found out that the dash brackets were breaking because when the vehicle went into a hole the chassis jolted and they were pulling on the dash.

A light cab was required to take a Commer chassis and I started to design a cab which was quite a nice shape; it had a sloping windscreen which saved me having to saw out all the roof places and wasting a lot of wood and time. I acquired some ash bent at a place in Ormskirk who specialised in bending and we used them when we built caravans. We had the ribs bent instead of sawing them out. I was then able to make up quite a light, but very strong, cab and I also introduced the idea of putting a panel on the outside which I shaped in the way of polished aluminium into a spear shape on the side and it looked very smart indeed when it was painted and the mouldings were polished, and, it was under the weight required. When the boss and the manager saw this they were delighted and we made quite a lot of these cabs.

The manager asked me if there was anything I needed and I told him that if we had a folding machine I would be able to fold instead of having to clamp pieces of wood on and then bash them with a hammer. He agreed to this; both the manager and the owner, were never afraid to ask me because they knew that I knew my job.

It was, however, quite a long procedure and I had seen a pneumatic hammer advertised for knocking out dints in mudguards. I suggested that we get one of these so we were able to get a portable model. You were then able to use it to beat out a wing. It was u-shaped and underneath would be the planishing block and on the top was a pneumatic hammer. I fitted this onto a stand so I could just beat the corner panels out roughly and then run them over on the pneumatic hammer. This meant that I was able to do them in minutes.

The only trouble was that it made a dreadful noise and as soon as I started the bodybuilders would shout at me so I had to beat a hasty retreat behind the wall where I was out of range. But it was a very interesting part of my work.

I was amazed at the amount of work this garage acquired in view of the fact that it was situated out in the country. They were the agents for various cars, including Citroen and Rover, and they also had 40 wagons. They were always very busy and we hardly ever had any drivers available. Sometimes the manager would come and say to me, 'I'm sorry to take you off your job, Percy, but would you like to deliver this wagon?' This was a nice change, of course, so I would just pack away my tools and get off before a driver came in.

One vehicle which they wanted to demonstrate was a new Thornycroft articulated lorry and I was the only person with a licence to drive an articulated vehicle. I had to go with the salesman to one of the mill towns to perform the demonstration. Another time I had to deliver a big eight-wheeler to North Wales; I was following a tram in

Bootle for such a long time and could not get past. The tram stopped and I pulled out to get past and as I came alongside the tram another tram came round the corner, right in front of me. I put my brakes on and nothing happened. The handbrake was on a ratchet and you had to ratchet it three or four times before it would tighten the cable so I hurriedly did this and I was then able to slow down and pull back behind the tram. When I looked at the vacuum guage, (they were vacuum brakes on the big wagons), there was no vacuum. I found out that as it had been running so slow for so long it had lost all its vacuum and you could not possibly press the brake without this vacuum as they were far too powerful. Overhauling them was quite a job, I can tell you.

One night one of the mechanics wanted a petrol tank repairing and I would never touch a tank until I had had water running through it for a while. He wanted it doing there and then but I told him that I was not going to do it. He was not very pleased. I went to carry on doing something else in another part of the works when all of a sudden there was a tremendous explosion. Apparently he had decided to solder it but there must have been some soot as he was using a very big iron which had got very hot and had ignited the gas in the tank. Of course, it blew the tank to pieces but fortunately he was unhurt. He had a black face and he could not hear very well as a result of the explosion, but it certainly taught him a lesson.

The boss wanted floodlights fixing outside the garage so Teddy and I fixed some up for him. A new road was going to be opened and the boss wanted the lights to be working when the road was opened. We were working in the pouring rain trying to get the lights working. They were so dim and we just could not get one of them to strike, so we tried all sorts of things. We wondered if the voltage was right and having a friend who was a foreman with Manweb, I telephoned him and he came round right away. Apparently we were on the end of the mains and the sodium lights would not strike up if they are not getting the correct voltage. He adjusted the mains on the main switchboard and we found that they certainly did not strike up. However, we were highly complimented on that particular job.

If you were working on a wagon on the road at the front of the garage at night, water rats would run across the road looking for food, and if you were lying down underneath one of the wagons they would run all over you. This wasn't a very nice experience.

I did not have much spare money at that time so I asked the manager if they would buy me a bike and let me pay it off in instalments. They did this and when it arrived one of the lads said, 'Oh, fancy buying one of those old things. It won't last you five minutes'. It was a three speed gear with Dunlop tyres and saddle. I rode that bike for years.

Chapter Eleven

Manning the Home Front

WAR BROKE OUT whilst I was at Woodwards. I decided to make a shelter in my house in Kew Road, Birkdale. I was in the fire brigade and I used to go out every eighth night. I asked permission to use the waste wood from the lorry park for shuttering for the shelter. Cement was also very scarce and there was a load of cement which had gone off in one corner of the garage, so every night I would find one or two bags that hadn't entirely gone off and I would take a tin full of cement home on the handlebars of my bike, until I had sufficient to enable me to do the brickwork on the side of the shelter. I bricked up the front and then I acquired some old bed irons and placed some shuttering under the roof and covered that over in concrete. It only came up to half the height of the kitchen, so it did not take off too much light. When I told one of the lads at work about the shelter he said, 'You windy so and so, the bombers will never get this far'. 'Don't you believe it, I was in the First World War and I know how far the bombers could go even then'. Now we were about twenty years in advance of the technology of the First World War. Of course, the bombers did come over and, in fact, some bombs were dropped very near to our house. So near, in fact, that one night the vibrations shook the whole house and the shutters fell down. Bombs first fell in Southport on 4th September 1940. A total of 17 people were killed and 12 houses totally demolished by bombs.

If there was an air raid at night time, my wife and our three children would go in the shelter and they would be nice and cosy. They never missed a night's rest, whereas other children had to be brought down out of their beds and go under the kitchen table. My children were sleeping more or less in comfort so all my work was not in vain.

I also decided to make a way out, so I knocked out a hole at the back of the house and made a tunnel into the garden where I had made another shelter. I dug a hole in the garden and put a roof over it and grassed it over and I then put a doorway on. I was going into the garden one day when I saw smoke coming out of the shelter. It smelt like cigarette smoke and when I opened the door I found two of my sons and two evacuees from Liverpool sitting puffing away on cigarettes!

We were all on a Ribble bus one time travelling to work. There was an awful lot of snow on the ground and the driver was trying to keep up to time. He kept slithering all over the road and eventually we got within about a mile of our destination when he went into a terrific skid. He only just managed to get out of it before the bus went over on its side and into a ditch. It was a double decker bus and as soon as we went into the skid I dived under the seat. We decided that we should walk the remainder of the journey and arrived at work just a little bit late.

My employers had a Leyland agency and I had to go one day to Leyland to pick up a new chassis. It was the very first model of a heavy goods vehicle, having two front axles and one at the rear. Another day I was sent out to a car that would not start two or three miles away. The battery cells had gone flat and I had to take out the floorboards to get at it. The battery was very badly corroded. The daughter of the house was waiting to go somewhere, so I decided that to get it started I would put a lead on from another battery, which I did. I needed somebody to press the starter pedal which was on the floorboard. This girl came out and she only had her nightie on and I asked her if she would be kind enough to press the starter pedal for me. She showed her lovely long bare leg and thigh – how on earth could a fellow concentrate on trying to start the engine with such a sight in touching distance. However, I knew I must not, because I could not risk getting the sack, but nevertheless what a great temptation!

The firm also took on a Citroen agency and a new model was delivered. Actually it was an entirely new way of building a mass-produced car, pioneered in the French factory. The body was built more or less out of pieces of tin welded together. It had front-wheel drive and torque suspension which was simply steel rods anchored at both ends and which, on taking uneven loads or whatever, would twist. The bar was made out of high tensile steel and it would twist in one direction and then it would recover itself, the same thing as a spring would do but very much more cheaply made.

The engine had detachable cylinder liners so that when a liner became very badly worn you simply pressed out the liner and fitted a new one in. It wasn't a separate chassis, it was fitted to the body, but Citroen supplied a stretching job with which to take the body off, (at least, the part would come off), and anchor it with long bolts into the stretching jig. It was attached to the suspension on the front and then by winding a handle on two long screws you were able to pull it back into shape again with the assistance of a few hammer blows. It was quite a novel thing in every way. When the demonstrator first came to us with this, he took us for a joy ride and he was doing nearly 70 mph. He turned up onto the pavement and ran along it to show us the spring system. A day or two later one of the salesmen took this Citroen out and decided to try to do the same. Unfortunately it ended up on its side in a ditch and he was lucky not to have drowned. I had to go out with a big first aid crane breakdown truck and lift the car out bodily.

I can remember having to go out to a wagon that had broken down quite a long way away. It had overturned on an island and was carrying hundreds of bottles. The firm had a contract with Fosters in Liverpool who made bottles. The chassis was all twisted but luckily I had taken the 'ambulance' which I had made to tow behind the breakdown wagon.

I had to lift one end of the chassis onto the breakdown towing ambulance and then lift the other end with the crane and go home very slowly. It took us several hours and it was quite a job straightening all that out. We had to get the bodybuilders to remove the body and the cab and we had to straighten out all the members but we fixed it in the end.

Some of the older Commer wagons had a kickup over the back axle and the chassis to make the chassis comparatively lower. They also had tipping bodies and sometimes if a driver came to tip his load and if he wasn't on an even keel, the thing used to just heel over and bend all the chassis. The boss sent for me the next time a twisted chassis came in and said, 'What do you suggest?' So I said, 'Well, I suggest that we straighten it with the oxyacetaylene and then fill the channel with hardwood, cut to shape and bolted on'. He thought that this was a good idea, so we did this and this forstalled a lot of trouble. Another thing that we had with the new Commers was the bolts shearing off in the axle shafts so I devised this idea of drilling out the hubs and the axle plates, drilling them out with a flat drill to form a recess then making some hardened steel washers which I would slip over two of the bolts. We never had any shearing off trouble after that, but the drivers were so very rough.

I was asked to do another interesting job. We were agents for Albions, and we had a tremendous big Albion chassis sent to us. The bodybuilders built the cab and it had a tanker body which I had to fit. They bought this tank and I fitted it, then I had to fit a pump to the engine to discharge the load, which I did, then I had to make a lot of brackets. I fitted the pump and then they wanted a trailer. I had to make all the towing things, it was a lovely job when it was finished, all nicely painted and lined, it was a tremendous vehicle.

A big haulage contractor from Manchester ordered a Leyland six wheeler and a new body and cab with trade plates on. I followed them to Manchester and when we pulled into his yard he came and said to me, 'You've been a hell of a long time haven't you? I understand that these diesel engines can be run out straight away'. 'Well, I am sorry, but I just happen to be one of the old-fashioned drivers and I do not like to punish a new vehicle.' 'Quite right lad, you are a good lad, come into the office'. He took me into the office and gave me a glass of beer, which, as a matter of fact, I did not like, and he also gave me ten bob and thanked me very much.

I only remember ever having one little argument with the boss. We were doing a wagon up to sell and, of course, he did not want to have to spend too much on it. One of the headlamps was badly damaged and he asked me if I would be able to repair it. I told him that I did not know as it was very badly damaged, but I would have a go. I took it to pieces and hammered it out and varnished it, but when I put the rim on it wasn't properly true so I put a glass in eventually and tried it on by forcing the rim on and cracked the glass. He came along just as I was doing this and he more or less accused me of being careless in cracking the glass which actually only cost a few coppers. However, I put some extra packing round the rim and put in another glass and it was alright, but that was the only time I had a disagreement with him.

However, there was one very funny incident involving him. The offices were up on the balcony and one of the clerks was a very nice lad, who, incidentally, was deformed. We would pull his leg and one day I was standing on the back of the platform of a cab doing some welding. I had my goggles on and I looked up at the balcony and I thought that this lad was looking out of the window. So I started pulling all kinds of faces and gestures to make him laugh, but when I took off my goggles it was the boss standing there.

The boss lived in a nice big detached house about a mile away and had a showroom and a paint shop. He fell out with the painter and asked me to go down and help. He wanted two or three cars touching up and respraying ready for reselling. It was quite a diversion from working in the factory.

Notices were put up in the works asking for volunteers to join either the NFS or the local territorials. I chose the NFS. I didn't realise at first, I thought that they were just doing it to protect the streets where we lived. However, there was pay attached to it and we signed up. Some of us went into the Territorials and the others went into the Fire Service. It was a volunteer brigade. They had a driver, but he could not always be on duty, and I was the only one with a licence to drive a fire engine. I had a PSV badge so I got the job of driving the fire engine whenever the regular driver couldn't. This was the biggest thrill of my life, driving a fire engine with an open windscreen and the bell clanging. It wasn't a very fast one, it was on solid tyres and had a very narrow track and when you had a crew of about 8 on board and 250 gallons of water, you had to take the corners very carefully. However, the people in the village were very thrifty and we seldom had a fire except occasionally in the pine woods. We practised pretty regularly, and being a volunteer brigade, it was pretty lacksadaisical. In fact, the chaps used to smoke whilst we were travelling around the streets. One Sunday we had an exercise and we went into the village where there was supposed to be a house on fire and smoke belching from it. I had to stay outside in case the pump was required with the engine. My mates dashed inside and they were coming out one by one with these lovely girls on their shoulders, so I thought to myself, I must have a go at this. I switched the engine off and went inside looking for someone who had been overcome by the smoke. The first room I went into there was this great big chap, about 19 stones, on the floor, under the window groaning. I took one look at him and immediately went looking elsewhere. It would have taken about three men to carry him out. When I was in the NFS I used to go on duty every eight days and sometimes I would take my uniform with me to work and change out of my working clothes into my uniform and then go and do my all night stint.

One winter's night I was changing into my uniform behind one of the benches. The NFS had a beautiful tunic which was made in Scotland. I had put on my tunic and my tin hat and my axe was on my belt, of course, and I had on my wellington boots but when I came to look for my trousers I could not find them.

Some of the fellows had hidden them (they were always playing jokes) and just as I was standing there, imploring them to bring me my trousers, the Boss's wife came in with her mother-in-law, to look around the works. She saw me standing there behind the bench and said, 'Oh, Percy, you do look lovely, come out and let us have a look at you'. I only had on little short underpants and my wellington boots and I looked most peculiar. I made some excuse not to go out and eventually the lads gave me back my trousers and I was able to go on duty.

By and large we did have quite a lot of fun with the brigade, until the bombs started to drop, then it became very hectic indeed. I was very fortunate in as much as I missed three really hair raising episodes. One was when the brigade was called out to a fire a couple of miles away. A car was on fire and when they arrived at the scene and opened the car door, a burning corpse fell out. A chap had committed suicide by setting fire to himself. Another night the police came and asked for a volunteer to go down with them to the railway as a chap had jumped in front of a train. The volunteer was asked to take a sack with him. The poor fellow was badly mutilated.

Then there was a call from Liverpool where there had been a big air raid, and one of the lads went with the fire engine and he was away for three days and nights. When he came back he was thoroughly tired and exhausted. One fire engine was completely enveloped when one of the warehouse walls fell on top of it. However, I also missed this particular episode.

The captain was always telling us that we were going to have a brand new fire engine delivered which would be capable of doing over 60 miles per hour, but right up until the time I left the brigade we had to make do with the Morris.

It was becoming quite dangerous travelling in the blackout to carry out my fireman's duties. It was particularly difficult to leave my wife and children but at least they had a shelter to go to. Despite all this mayhem there were some nights, when I was pedalling home, when I looked back at Liverpool and saw a circle of search lights weaving in the sky and couldn't help thinking they looked very pretty.

We had taken in so many vehicles in part exchange that the paint shop could not cope with the repainting. The manager asked me if I knew anyone who could help to paint them and make them look presentable. I thought that perhaps my father may be interested, so I asked him and he was delighted.

I drove the first one home, it was a big eight wheeler. He cleaned it all up, sandpapered it and made quite a presentable job of painting it in two colours. Then he decided to line it but I'm afraid he wasn't very good at it and it looked pretty awful. I was rather embarrassed when I took it back but the boss said that it was alright, they would soon get rid of it.

I was working outside the garage one afternoon, when I heard a number of aircraft approaching. When I looked up there was a complete squadron flying in formation. Suddenly one of them attempted to land in what he must have thought was a flat field, but there was a very deep and narrow ditch running across it which apparently he had not seen when he was approaching. When he hit the ditch he bounced up in the air – it must have been about 20 or 30 feet – and then he landed upright. Luckily he was unhurt. He came to the garage and asked if he could use the telephone. He rang Woodvale and told them that he was with a certain squadron and that he had crash landed and could they please send someone out. We asked him what had happened but he was very non-committal and wouldn't even tell us where they came from. Eventually a guard from the RAF regiment came, but the plane remained in the ditch for a few days. The legs and the undercarriage were badly damaged and they had to get replacement parts. When they had repaired it, they towed it out of the field and onto the main road. A pilot, warrant officer and flight engineer came along and got inside the plane and eventually started it up. They held up the traffic whilst the plane took off in a northerly direction. We never actually found out where he was going to

I became very friendly with a chap who wrote our insurance claims and I would go with him on an insurance job and tell him what I thought about it, for example, how long it would take to repair and we worked very well together.

As for my regular job, I did not like having to work on a Saturday night, travelling in the blackout all the time and then having to travel to the fire brigade as well. I had seen an advert in Southport for toolmakers so I went along for an interview. They agreed to take me on, so, very reluctantly, I gave in my notice. They did not want me to leave but fully understood that being a family man it was far better for me to get a job nearer home.

Chapter Twelve

Business in the Driving Seat

WHEN WE WERE in business we had two sets of trade plates, one set was £5, and called a limited version, and the other set was £25 a year and called general plates. On one occasion I went on a holiday with my wife in an old model T Ford. We went to Wales and we had general trade plates on. (If you went out with the cheaper limited plates on you had to carry a chit which had been made out in the office and a copy would be kept in the office together with all the relevant details.)

We had just had a lovely day out when a police constable pulled us up and asked me what we were doing. I told him that I was on holiday. He wanted to know if I was demonstrating the vehicle or taking it to be sold. I informed him that I was definitely on holiday. So he said, 'Very good, but I will have to take a few particulars'.

He even took the colour of my eyes and I received a summons to appear in Bangor, which is quite a long way away from Southport. I went to Bangor and when it came to my turn there was a minister on the bench and a lady. The public prosecutor made it look very dark for me; the fact that I had used the trade plates for holiday purposes. I was fined £5 and had my licence endorsed, but if I had told the policeman that I was demonstrating the vehicle he could not have done a thing about it, but I told him the truth and was fined for my candour.

I wrote to the national trade journals and warned all traders about this because everyone, naturally, was purchasing general trade plates at £25, thinking that they were saving money. In future if anyone was asked what they were doing, they always said they were on business not pleasure.

When I went down to London to pick up a chassis I had to take quite a lot of ready cash with me. We travelled on the mail train and there would be pickpockets and con men on board. A friend and I were travelling on the train and he was set upon. He had a tiny revolver which he took out and he took a shot at the man who was trying to rob him. Happily, he missed and shot a hole through the carriage window.

I had a big German revolver which I kept in my pocket whenever I went down to London. On one of these journeys a very shady-looking character got into my compartment and kept looking at me over the top of his newspaper, pretending to be reading. It was common knowledge that if a person was carrying trade plates with them invariably it meant they would be carrying money. This was an open invitation to thieves.

This particular man kept eyeing me up so I just pulled my jacket back and showed the tip of the revolver. He had a good look at this and I think he must have decided that I was no mug because he got up and went into another compartment, probably to try again on someone else.

I didn't always travel by train, however, and I remember one occasion when I was travelling out of London in a car and people kept waving to me. I thought to myself, 'It's all very well you laughing and waving at me, I have to do 230 miles sitting on a reconditioned Italian chassis and box by Ferrari, on a 20-gallon petrol tank, dressed in an old flying suit, cap and cape'. A motorist then went past and shouted, 'Do you know you are on fire?' I hopped off and looked underneath. The footbrake was underneath the petrol tank and it must have been adjusted too tightly and the friction had caused it to light the grease which was merrily blazing away. I was able to take off my hat and beat out the flames with it, but it could have been very nasty indeed.

One day I was travelling down Lord Street in a heavy wagon when a policeman on point duty blew his whistle as I went past him. I stopped and he came up to me and said, 'Do you know you are covering up your rear number plate?' I answered that I hadn't known. I went round the back to have a look and the backboard had dropped down and was covering up the number plate. He could see very well that I wasn't doing this on purpose, and I simply had to lift the board up and put the hook on again. However, he booked me and I had to go to court. When the magistrate asked me why I was driving along with my number plate obscured, I told him that if there had not been so many holes in the road, (Lord Street was then paved with wooden blocks and in places had become worn) the back would not have dropped down and I would not have been covering my plate up. However, they did not have any sympathy with me and I was fined £2.

I had another brush with the law when Southport's football team was playing at home and we ran coaches from our house which was about a mile and a half away from the ground. We used to charge a shilling a head. One day I set off with a 14-seater coach and as I was driving along fellows who were late for the match would hop on and when I arrived at the ground the assistant inspector, Bob Smith, counted the passengers getting off and when they had all unloaded he came up to me and asked me if I knew how many passengers I had on board. I told him that I had had 14 when I left the house. So he told me that when I arrived at the ground I had 26 on board. I told him that I could not help it, I was simply driving along and people just jumped on when I slowed down at the corners, but there again the magistrate thought it was a very serious offence and I was fined again.

Early on, we had two wagons working on contract and they were carting sludge to the farmers. One morning I had to go out to one that would not start. I went on my motor bike which I had done up very nicely. I had made some aluminium discs for the wheels and some aluminium mudguards and had put a long brass exhaust pipe on it because it was a twin-cylinder engine. The exhaust was a siren which Daimler vehicles were fitted with. It was an exhaust almost like a ship's siren, but the police in some areas said it was illegal to use. However, I had obtained one of these sirens and fitted it to my motor bike and it made a lovely gurgling sound.

One morning at about 5 a.m. I was going down Lord Street, in Southport, riding my motorbike with both hands in the pockets of my old army coat, when suddenly I saw a stick appear. A police sergeant was at the other end of it and he stopped me and said, 'Do you think this is a race track?' 'There's nobody about,' I said. However, I apologised and he let me go.

At this time the police were following vehicles on motor bikes and side cars testing the speed at which they were travelling. But there were one or two crashes so the Police brought out a timing device and this made driving a misery because you had to keep to the speed limit which at that time was 20 m.p.h.

Whilst my father was still struggling in business with the one coach, we had several unfortunate incidents. On one occasion a driver, who turned out to be rather lax, went to Blackpool with a coach party. He pulled up outside a cafe and did not put the engine into gear and when the passengers alighted it rolled forward and smashed through a glass window. Fortunately this was the only damage caused. We discovered the reason for this accident when we examined the coach. The handbrake was connected by rods to the back axle and we found that as the passengers alighted and the load decreased, the springs returned to normal and this would let the brake off. This was why we always had to put the engine into gear whenever we stopped.

Another time he parked the coach on an incline and got out and went to talk to one of the passengers. Suddenly he heard a crash and the coach had run down the hill and hit some outside toilets. A poor old chap was sitting in one of them at the time and the toilets were nearly demolished, but miraculously he was unhurt. This was a big set back for my father who, had to pay to put it right.

This same driver came home another night with the engine thumping due to the fact that the bearing had gone. He had run it without oil and father had booked the coach for a trip to Wembley to the F.A. Cup Final the next Saturday. Of course, it was too late to get another coach or to do anything about it. When I came home father met me and told me about it. I said that there was nothing for it but to take the engine out and re-metal the bearings, and on this particular engine that meant that the steering column had to be removed. This created a lot of extra work but on the first night we took the engine out and father re-metalled the bearings. The following day and evening when I came home from work I started to scrape the bearing in and eventually we got it fitted.

I sent one of the lads who had been helping me round the block just to make sure that it was alright. He hadn't gone very far before there was a terrific noise underneath. I had left him to put the brake rods back on but he had forgotten to put a split pin in the front brake rod. Of course, it soon fell off onto the floor and was crumpled up into a terrible shape. I could have cried when it came back. We had to light the smithy fire and get it hot and straighten it out again. When the driver went down to Wembley I told him that he would have to go very carefully so that father would be able to get paid for this job.

One of our coaches broke down one night just outside London and I had to go down to bring it back. I had fitted a substantial towing bar to one of our vans. The driver of the coach was called Bill Glover and he was also a part-time footballer for Southport Football Club. (He once scored seven goals in one match, which in those days was a record, and so all the drivers used to address him by saying, 'Give it to Glover'. He admitted himself that on that particular day he should have scored twenty goals.) However, after filling up with petrol we set off again. We had travelled quite a few miles when I noticed that he had the headlights on and I could see that they were wobbling quite a bit. I stopped and he told me that he just could not keep awake and that he kept nodding off. I told him that I thought that we had better pull in, so we pulled off the road, had a smoke and got down on the coach floor to have a sleep. We had only just got off to sleep when somebody came and knocked us up. It was another coach driver, on his way to London with a load, wanting to know if we were alright. Unfortunately, after having been disturbed we just could not get back off to sleep. Nevertheless, Bill felt somewhat refreshed so we were able to set off again. After a while we came upon a transport cafe, so we pulled in and they let us have a wash in some lovely rainwater. We then had ham, eggs and toast and eventually arrived home.

One Saturday when Southport were playing in a cup tie, in 1931, at Goodison Park, Everton, I had to pick up a load of workers from the Vulcan Motor Works, Crossens, and there had been snow on the ground. We set off but we must have got water in the carburettor because I just could not keep the engine going. It kept spitting back and the passengers were becoming very anxious that we were not going to arrive at the match in time for the kick-off. They kept shouting at me, 'Go on driver, get it going!' and they were getting rather impatient. (They need not have been in such a hurry, for Southport was thrashed 9-1, thanks to that goal-scoring machine Dixie Dean.)

I did not have time to stop to clear out the carburettor, but when we arrived at the ground I was able to take the carburettor chamber off and sure enough there was water in it. I cleaned it out and put it back. On the way back I thought to myself, 'Well, I'd better let these motor mechanics see what our Pulmans can do'. So I put my foot down until they were shouting out for me to go easy because I was giving them rather a rough ride.

Amongst our fleet was an old Vulcan 26-seater and one Saturday the driver had to take a load to Yorkshire. After lunch I received a call from him saying that two of his back tyres had burst and would I go out to him and take some new tyres.

When I got to the coach I had to take off the wheels and I then tried to get the old tyres off. It was such a long time since they had been taken off that they were literally glued on to the wheel rim. We tried several ways of getting them off, including, sledge hammers and crow bars but we just could not get them off. The driver had the idea of sawing through the tyres so he went along to a nearby farm and borrowed the farmer's hand saw and we were then able to cut through the tyres quite easily. However, the tyres had steel wires embedded in the rubber around the rim. When he tried to saw through these he broke all the teeth on the saw, and then to make matters worse, he pulled a gate post up to use as a battering ram. It took us an awful long time to change these tyres!

When I was a young boy I used to go to the open air swimming pool which was at the other end of town. I can remember going there one day to have a swim. The water was grey because it was full of disinfectant to kill off any germs so you could not see how deep the water was. I got undressed and said to one lad, 'Which is the deep end?' 'This is it,' he said, pointing to where I was standing. So I dived in, but it was the shallow end and there was only 18 inches of water. I scraped all down my chest and lost one of my socks into the bargain. I went home very dejected. What funny ideas some people have of a joke!

My elder brother was a great pigeon fancier and at the weekends he never wanted to have to drive his coach. It got so that the other drivers resented having to do jobs which he should have been doing, and in the end it got to such a pitch that father and I had a talk about it and decided that the only thing to do was to give him the coach and let him work on his own account. We did this, letting him drive a brand new coach which was worth about £900 at the time. We found out at a later date that more and more new coaches were being put on the road and he was missing out on work. Eventually, he sold his coach and went to work for a coach firm. It was his job to take girls to the ammunition works in Liverpool, and one day he was travelling along a familiar road when he saw a tram coming towards him which should not have been there. Naturally this rather confused him. Regrettably, the tram crashed into the side of his coach, setting fire to it and sadly killing several of the girls. My brother was badly injured and it turned out that the driver of the tram was a young boy who had taken the tram for a lark. This caused an awful lot of damage and it really upset my brother to hear the girls screaming.

His son, who was in the R.A.F., was coming down one night to see his gran before going back off leave. He had a Morris sports car, but the dynamo wasn't charging properly, and he had asked me to have a look at it for him. I told him that I would, but for some reason I wasn't able to find time to have a look at it, so he used his motor bike instead. It was a dark night and as he was coming down the road to go to his gran's house, he crashed into the corner of a brick shelter which was at the side of the road. The first thing we knew about it was when the infirmary telephoned to tell us about the accident. My brother asked me if I would go the the infirmary with him. We went on our bikes, expecting to be able to sit and talk with him. However, when we arrived at the infirmary the sister met us and told us that his injuries were serious and that there was no hope for him. This was a terrible shock and tragically he died within minutes of us getting to the infirmary. I will never forget the grief of my brother and his wife when we got back home. It turned out at the inquest that it had been a taxi driver who had caused him to crash into the shelter. I had come to treat my nephew as one of my own and it was a dreadful shock when the accident happened. At the graveside the R.A.F. were very good about it and they sent several aeroplanes over, they dipped in salute, but nevertheless it was a very sad occasion for us all.

On another occasion I remember going to pick up an old bus called a Hupmobile, which we were taking in part exchange from Newmarket. It was in a shocking state and I had a job to start it. However, eventually I got it started and when I arrived in Nottingham it was lunchtime and people were coming out from work. I had to stop on a busy crossroads and the engine conked out. The battery was no good and I could not get it started using the starting handle because the engine was very hot. As I was holding up the traffic, some chaps came up to me and asked me if I would like a push. I was reluctant to sit in whilst they pushed so I got out and steered with one hand whilst they pushed. They pushed so hard that they got quite a speed up and when the engine started I only just had time to dash in through the door and grab the steering wheel, and turn the bus round the corner before putting the brakes on. If I hadn't done this there would have been a nasty accident because the road was crowded with people. I had to stay the night in Nottingham and I pulled into a wayside cafe which also had chalets. They fixed me up for the night and I got chatting to a very nice young waitress who had served me my meal. I was very tired, so I went to bed and fell asleep straight away. However, the next morning she brought my breakfast and said, 'Oh, I expected you last night, I left my bedroom window open'. Of course, this did not impress me very much because I had a good wife and family.

Another time I was bringing in an open coach, high speed model of a Lancia. I was coming round a corner and the steering locked and I just could not straighten it out. I was within six miles of home and I found that I had only got one left lock and the other side of the steering was locked straight ahead. I thought of a way home whereby I could go round left hand corners and this is what I did. Sometimes I had to reverse to get an extra lock on but in the end I arrived home safely. When I examined it, I took the steering box to pieces and found that it was very badly worn and that a nut had come off inside and locked itself between the worm and the wormwheel.

Chapter Thirteen

Mannings move from strength to strength

I ALWAYS enjoyed working in my little workshop at the bottom of the garden so around Christmas time I decided to make some dominoes in my spare time, as they were difficult to obtain just after the war. I managed to get hold of a sheet of bakelite which cost me £8, and I cut it into domino-sized shapes and I used my buffing machine to buff them up. I made a template to drill the requisite number of spotted holes. I used the finishing machine to cut the dominoes. Then at night time my wife and my mother would help me to paint the dots. I then purchased some tea chests and cut them up and made some boxes to pack the dominoes in. One of my wife's uncles sold ink and writing materials to retail shops so he was able to sell some of these dominoes for me. When the first consignment was sold I wanted to buy some more materials but I just did not have enough money.

About two months before this particular Christmas, I decided to make some dolls' houses because they too were very scarce. I obtained several tea chests and with the equipment I had already purchased I was able to make a gross of dolls' houses, each about 18" tall by 18" wide, with four bedrooms and a staircase. I purchased metal dolls house fittings and my mother and my wife helped me to wallpaper the houses and put 'brick' paper on the outside. It was quite a nice job when they were finished.

I came across a chap who travelled around selling toys and he took all the dolls houses off my hands. He paid me way below top price but at the time we were educating our sons and we needed the money badly.

At this time there was no such thing as Meccano, but I obtained a small press, made some press tools and a little bench shearing machine. I was then able to buy a lot of nuts and bolts and various off-cuts of metal. I had the idea of making an overhead crane, much like those now created using Meccano. The crane consisted of a tower with a long, revolving section overhead with a running track on it and it was worked by hand, of course. I made little handles and then I made a compressor out of an ex-army pump which was fitted onto a gearbox, then I fitted it onto a base and put a pulley onto it. By this time the authorities were changing over from DC to AC and they came to visit me to see what I had. When I showed them they informed me that it was illegal. I told them that this may be so, but it served my purposes, and that if they were going to change the current then I would want some form of compensation.

They agreed to let me have all new motors if I fitted them and naturally I jumped at the chance. They supplied the new motors and I was able to motorise the machines. AC worked much better - DC motors would get hot and I would have to wait for them to cool down. I obtained a printer to enable me to print boxes with colourful pictures on, then managed to get paper to pack up all the contents and, finally, little envelopes for the nuts. I had a lot of help from my family on these projects. I ran out of paint and so I was not able to finish the cranes. All I needed was £30, so I asked my brother if he would lend me the money. Unfortunately he would not and so I was unable to finish off the cranes in time for Christmas. I had made arrangements for them to be sold and I was to receive 30/- for each set which at that time was quite a lot of money.

When I decided to start up on my own I knew that there was a shortage of iron gates. I knew how to make them and I also had most of the machinery required, with the exception of a welder. I was able to buy an electric welder from a steel merchant who supplied the old firm. I got in touch with them and they also agreed to let me have the metal I needed. Across the road from my house there was an ex-smithy, complete with bellows. I was able to rent this for half a crown a week which was a very good start indeed. My son drew the designs and I began making gates. He came to help me during his first vacation from university and on the Monday morning one of the lads dropped a piece of heavy metal on his big toe and broke it. It did not bother him at all and he hobbled about on it for about a week or two until it healed. I was always afraid of him hurting his hands as he was training to be a doctor, which he is now. I built up quite a good business making gates and we had managed to save quite a bit of money.

I could not afford a motor vehicle, but I had my bike which I had bought some time previously and I fitted a trailer to it. I called upon one of the ex-directors of the firm I used to work for and he asked me to make him a pair of gates and posts. The day I delivered them to his house, it was raining and so, upon arrival, I was soaked. He said to me, 'Why don't you buy a little motor vehicle?' But I replied, 'Well, I will as soon as I can afford to, but I just cannot at the moment'. He then offered to act as guarantor for a £200 overdraft, but the bank rejected this, and so he lent me the money! He gave me £200 and I bought a little old Bedford van for £25. The chassis had all rotted away, so my son set to with me and we soon re-plated all the chassis with the welder which I had been able to afford and we made it quite presentable. The engine used to oil the plugs up and it needed re-boring but unfortunately, I could not afford to do this so we simply cleaned the plugs.

My middle son had now joined up and served his time as a car body repairer under a very experienced boss. Although he was exempt, he still wanted to do his National Service and signed on for three years in the R.E.M.E. He went out to Korea when the war was on and had a pretty rough time living, eating and sleeping in the same tent. When he came home and I met him at Liverpool Station in my little old Bedford van, my wife and I were so delighted and pleased to see him safely back that I decided to ask him if he would like to come into business with me, which I am pleased to say he did. We formed a partnership, doing body repairs and we soon became very busy with this. As a result, we had to build an extension to the works which were proving to be too small for us to carry out car repairs as well. I asked the owner of the property if I could erect the extension, but he was not too happy about it as he had been thinking about increasing the rates, but I told him that if he increased the rates I would be happy to pay them. We needed a three phase cable installing down the entry – I think the cost was about £90. However, the owner of the premises suggested that he should pay half, which he duly did. The cable was very useful to us because by this time I had bought a big second-hand lathe which was also a milling machine.

I desperately wanted to get back into engineering and so I fitted the lathe and the milling machine and as a result we took on the job of overhauling a children's roundabout from the fairground. I had to make new bevelled gearwheels for it and we did not have facilities on the milling machine to make gears, so I turned up the shape of the pinion, then drilled and marked it out. I drilled a lot of holes where the teeth were going to be and then I sawed them all out with a hacksaw and filed it all nicely. We finished up with quite a nice gearwheel.

Another of our customers, who was also a very old friend, had a Rover car and he would come at all sorts of odd times and want little bits of welding doing. As my son was working on the car the chap said, 'I know somebody who wants some coil springs making, would you be interested?' I informed him that we were interested in making anything which made us an honest living, so the following day he arrived with nine coils of wire, the idea being that I would use 44 feet of this to make a coil, which was about an inch outside diameter. It was 3/16th nickel chrome wire. I thought about how to do it on my old lathe and I took a piece of solid fibre, mounted it on the sliding tool post and cut off 44 feet. I set the lathe in bottom gear and gradually wound it along by hand, which was a very laborious job. However, we made the initial samples and fixed a reasonable price for them. This developed into a big order.

We were by this time getting a lot of work and the yard was becoming somewhat cluttered. So we decided that we would have to look for larger premises and as we did not have much capital, we decided to go and see the bank manager.

In fact, he came and visited us at the works to see what we were making and what the potential was. He agreed to lend us money to enable us to obtain more property and my son and I had to give our personal guarantees. We managed to obtain one of the old buildings which our old firm had owned prior to going into liquidation. It cost us about £2,500 but when we had first bought it in 1920 we had paid £225 for a pair of cottages and ground. By this time we were obtaining heavy engineering work and we decided that an overhead crane would come in very handy. I went to various scrap yards in Liverpool and eventually I found a complete overhead crane which I bought very reasonably for about £25. It had a 30 cwt. capacity which at the time was sufficient, but we had to buy new runners – 6 by 3 RSJs – to make a runway the length of the works, and we altered the length of the carriageway which proved very handy.

We kept one or two chaps doing nothing other than making gates, which was quite a lucrative business. We were able to knock them out in no time at all and my son would go around fitting them. In the end we acquired so much general engineering work that we had to cut out the car repair work completely.

One night we had a break-in and I had a large safe about 4 feet by 3 feer which was situated in the small office we had constructed. They had cut a hole in the safe, opened the door and taken out about £100 together with a number of stamps. Worse than that, they set fire to a lot of papers in my office – there were a lot of invoice copies burnt. Out of spite they broke some of the vehicles' mirrors and cut open some of the tool boxes belonging to the lads and generally did a lot of damage.

By this time we were in a position to purchase a second hand car. My son purchased a Rover, a pretty old model, and we spent quite a lot of money on it, overhauling it, and in the end it proved to be a very reliable car. I borrowed it on one occasion to go on holiday to Wales. We wanted some sort of transport for the business though, so I bought a Hillman pick-up which we overhauled, modernised and fitted with a tow bar – we were then able to have holidays in the caravan towed by the Hillman.

Father had attended a sale at Rhyl where there were some army huts available. Because we wanted to build a larger works, we bought some of the huts and I took three or four of the lads to the empty camp. As we had only two crowbars between us I decided to make some more out of spring steel. When we started taking the nails from out of the roof we found that the two crowbars I had made were simply buckling the corrugated iron and more often than not, were not pulling out the nails. We were taking it all to the railway station, as at that time it was more economical to send things by rail rather than by wagon. We had signed an agreement that we would completely clear the area when we dismantled the huts and came across one that had been used by the Women's Army Corp as a bath house. I had seen graffiti in the men's toilets, but my word, I had never seen anything like the graffiti we found on the walls of this bath house!

One building was the rifle range and the end of it was bricked up. However, this wall was the last thing to be taken down and when we came to dislodge the bricks, we found that rather than the bricks coming away from the mortar, we were simply breaking them. They had been set in cement and it was almost impossible to get them apart. I telephoned my father and he told me that we would just have to leave them, which we did and luckily heard no more about the matter. Whoever came after us to clear the site would have had to have used explosives to move them.

We had just got the buildings ready and the machinery installed when a gentleman, who was a cotton broker, approached my father and said that he would like to take an interest in the business. We had indeed spent a great deal of money, so father agreed that he should put £1,000 into the business and we started to work in this building. Father insisted on keeping the existing works operational, which was a good thing because this gentleman proved to be greedy and kept suggesting that we move our existing works to the new building. Father simply would not do this, and in the end he became rather nasty and said that he wanted his money back. Of course, this proved to be difficult for us as it was not easy to borrow money from a bank. However, we struggled on and withdrew completely from the new building. We lost money on this deal and eventually the building was sold and then demolished.

Chapter Fourteen

Reminiscences

WHEN I commenced work in Southport during the war, the boss was not very well acquainted with engineering, although he was a tremendous salesman. I remember saying to him once that I had been reading about a new vehicle agency that was being put on the market. I said 'I suppose you will be taking on the agency for this new car?' 'No, not yet, I'll wait until somebody else takes it on, tries it out, and if it proves successful, then I'll take it over', he said. He had such a big sales turnover that he could have done this, but there was no doubt that he had tremendous business acumen. He did not have any hobbies but just came to work each morning and looked through the *Financial Times,* as he dedicated all his time to making money.

During my time there I overhauled quite a few cars, including one of the old Jaguars which had long, sloping mudguards which also served as a stepboard. I think it was called an SS and it had twin carburettors fitted. However, eventually they took me over into the toolroom where they had installed several new machines. They had a long overhead main shaft and were driving the various machines with belting. However, we were getting new machines so I rewired the place by installing three phase mains and motorising some of the existing milling machines. We were then able to dispose of the long shafting and all the belts and it certainly proved to be more economical. We were on contract to the Air Ministry making highly developed tools, and as this was an A1 priority listing, we were able to get any machine we needed.

One particular occasion, when we were tipping the tools with high speed steel, which was quite a long job, we used the acetylene process. We also obtained a But welder and I came to do the job. It was a very heavy consumption and I had to get special cable and put in an extra main switch. The local electrical suppliers could not supply the cable and so the boss got it from the Air Ministry. I wired the welder, tested it out and found that unit was very efficient. However, as time went on, we found that the tips on the tools were getting small surface cracks and decided that it was as a result of the metal being heated too quickly, so we had to stop using the welder and revert back to using the oxyacetylene welding process.

Part of the job, was heat treatment and this was something with which I was conversant, having worked in the smithy. I had fitted oven surfaces to two of them. One was an ordinary gas oven which only went up to about 500 or 600 degrees, which was more than adequate for some of the jobs, but steel had to have a much higher temperature so I had to fit a blower-assisted furnace which created a tremendous heat. I had to use a three-inch gas main to supply this furnace – I could not get any three-inch elbows for the gas pipes. I had to make some elbows by cutting them in a straight section of pipes, bending them over and welding them up. I would sometimes stand and watch the meters on the gas ticking over at a tremendous rate. There were not a lot of new machines available at that time and so we were able to buy some automatic lathes, but they were belt-driven as were some of the drilling and milling machines.

We were also making parts for the Blenheim Bomber. We forged 'T' pieces, but as they were of a very hard metal we had to get some special lubricant. We also put threads on the 'T' pieces.

As there was an awful lot of welding work to be done, I attended the local technical school in the evenings and was able, eventually, to perform some very intricate work. I was looking through an aeroplane book after the war and it showed a 'secret' unit which I had been making, at the school – it was simply for testing aero-engine gearboxes on take off.

We obtained two American machines and the first to arrive was a cylinder grinder which had a generating set called a Ward Lenard system. It alternated the AC current to DC because some of the motors were adjustable on this machine. When I came to look at the drawings they were actually in German, and, obviously, this was of no use to me and it took me a long time to sort out the wiring on this particular machine. However, I did it, and it worked and produced lovely grindings. Then we had a large jig borer delivered which was called a Newhall and was one of the very first large jig borers. It was delivered one Sunday morning and as we had no facilities for lifting it they got in touch with the RAF who sent two cranes down to unload it. The wagon drew from underneath and I had put some sleepers on the roadway outside. Unfortunately the crane drivers began to make errors. One was paying out when he should have been lifting and vice versa, and as the machine was about 8 feet high and weighed 7 tons, it was gradually tipping over. The driver on the wrong wire was accelerating instead of stopping and all of a sudden the machine crashed down onto the roadway. The drivers immediately went round to the front of the vehicle to have a quick discussion and decided to say that the clutch had slipped, which I knew was not the case. I surveyed the damage and the boss said to me 'What do you think?' I told him that I thought it could be repaired. Actually it had broken the castings around the top and one of the bearings was affected which took me three weeks to repair.

I got a man from the works in Peterborough to come and test the jig borer which proved to be doing its job to within a tenth of a thousand of an inch. As a result of this, I received a substantial rise in my salary without even asking for one. I installed it in one corner of the toolroom and it started working.

I had the idea of putting the generator outside in a building which had been specially made to house the jig borer and that made it all the better. It was later found that one or two of the jobs which it produced were not accurate. It turned out that the sunshine was expanding one side - overhead shades rectified that particular problem.

One day a chap who worked on the shaping machines came to me grumbling because he had got a shock off the inspection lamp which was fitted to the machine. Some of the wiring had been done before my time and the bulb had gone. He had put his finger in the holder for some reason and although it was switched off, he still received a terrific shock. That was soon fixed.

We had a very big lathe delivered which we were going to use for turning large items and also for broaching. I installed it and on doing a test piece found that it was about five thousands of an inch out in a turning six inches long. I took the shaft out and laboriously rescraped the bearings, replaced the shaft and tested it for alignment and in the end I managed to get it working perfectly.

We used to make press tools for the Lucas Factory in Burnley and were invited to the works one day. Most of us attended and as they had mainly girls working on the machines, most of the fellows were more interested in them than in the actual machinery!

One aspect I recall was the making of the ammunition belts for Spitfires and another interesting job was concerned with Blenheim bombers. The escape hatches on these planes had proven to be too small for the pilots to escape from if they were hit. We had orders to make new hatch covers very quickly as delivery was being held up. We made a jig for the new hatches and subsequently we were highly commended by the Air Ministry for doing it so quickly.

Returning from a day out to Liverpool Zoo by train, we suddenly heard a terrific bang. The train had been damaged by hitting a wagon and it had set on fire. Eventually the train stopped and we had to get off and walk to the nearest station, which was Crosby. We had to wait there for another train to come and take us back home to Southport. We found out later that the wagon had been driven by a boy who was so excited over driving it that he had not looked to see if there a train coming.

One time I was bringing a bus home as a part exchange and as it took longer than we expected to get home, darkness fell and we found we had no lights. I had with me a chap called Sammy Wit, he was wit by name and wit by nature. If you were out with Sammy you would never be stuck for anything. He went to a grocers in the village and bought some candles which he then proceeded to place inside the bus; one each side of the windows, one at the front and one at the back, but of course, the back one did not glow red, nor did it illuminate the number plate. Eventually we were stopped by a policeman and he asked us about the candles. When we explained what had happened he did not book us but he said, 'You might get stopped again before you get to Birkdale; if you do, tell them that I have already stopped you and decided not to take any action because of the circumstances'. However, we arrived safely home without any further incidents.

My younger brother was very fond of flying and he was friendly with a local pilot who provided pleasure flights. Every morning he had to fly over Blackpool to obtain a safety certificate, bearing in mind that he was carrying passengers. Needless to say my brother went with him.

One day a local circus came to a field near to our works and my brother went down for the first flight of the day which cost him 10/-. They got in and the pilot started up the engine but when they took off there was a lot of long grass and they caught a wire fence on the undercarriage which tipped the plane up onto its nose and subsequently it flipped over onto its back. Fortunately my brother was unhurt apart from a bruised nose and a slight cut on his head. The plane, however, was a total write off.

When my son and I began heavy engineering we made our youngest son, who was a landscape gardner, a tipping wagon which he used for quite a while until he decided that he wanted a bigger vehicle and bought a seven tonne Bedford. I had the idea of making a breakdown wagon which would more or less pick up a wreck or a breakdown on the same principle as the skips you can now hire to take away rubbish. I made two long rams along the side of the chassis and then I placed a heavy crossbar across the back, make a body for it and I used the hydraulic pump off the gearbox which we had on the tipping wagon. The pump consisted of two new cylinders and I made a body. The idea was that if there was an accident on a motorway, the driver could back up to it and load the vehicle onto the wagon without having to get out of his cab. He could then operate the hydraulic and it would lift up, deposit it on the chassis and they could then simply drive away. The other good thing about it was that there was no rubbish, oil or broken glass or anything left in the roadway which often happens when they are towing a vehicle away. This system would have been ideal in the Liverpool tunnel for getting broken down vehicles away quickly.

We made enquiries the following year regarding breakdown vehicles to the Mersey Tunnel, but they were not very interested. The local police, however, were very interested indeed. We had fitted these vehicles out with fire extinguishers, rubbish tips, brushes, shovels, sand and numerous other things required for breakdowns. We also had enquiries from abroad. However, in the end the breakdown wagon was simply cut up for scrap.

My eldest son, who was at university, and one of his friends had the great idea of making a telescope as they were very interested in the stars. They asked me to help them and as they were making their own condensers and lens I obtained some one-inch-thick glass, six inches in diameter which they began to grind up whilst I made other parts. We started by buying an air raid shelter which we erected in our garden. The telescope was to run round on a pivot so I went to the local scrap yard and acquired a rim off one of the fairground bumper cars. It was circular, about five feet in diameter and my son bolted this to the top of the shelter and we made wheels to run round the rim. Then he made a centre part, bolted it on and managed to get it to revolve. We then built a sort of shed with a top which opened out. He became very busy with his university work after that so he postponed the idea because of his studies.

One of the happiest moments of our lives came when we went to the Philharmonic Hall in Liverpool, to see him receive his degrees. It was a marvellous sight to see all the brightly-coloured cloaks and costumes belonging to the different professors. Our son had on his cap and gown and we saw him go up to collect his degrees. After the ceremony he took us out for a meal to celebrate.

Our youngest son eventually joined an R.A.F. regiment, even though he was exempt due to his work on the farm. We went to see his passing out parade which was a nice occasion, but unfortunately couldn't go to see our middle son's passing out parade as that was in Dorset.

When I worked at the engineering works one of the jobs I was given was to fit an air extracting plant over the grinding machines to take away the dust. I made joints and couplings in the overhead pipe system and one of the joints looked just like the shape of a pair of pants. One of the girls came along and said, 'What are you making?' I explained to her that I was making metal knickers for the night workers. She actually believed me and said, 'Oh, I'm not going to wear them!'

Chapter Fifteen

From Southport to Anglesey

WHEN we started making items for a company called Cooper Electroheat (about 1957) they had been experimenting quite a lot and Mr Cooper came up with the idea of making a metal S-shaped container to accommodate two electrical resistance coils. We made them out of two inch by quarter inch steel and they were used to preheat various heavy fabrications. We discovered that after one or two heats they were scaling very badly and the cost was high as there was quite a lot of work attached in making them. I suggested that we used three by one half inch channel which accommodated two double length coils. We did this and as a result this brought manufacturing cost down tremendously. But there was still a lot of scaling with the constant heating and cooling, so I suggested that we make them out of stainless steel and this we did. Mr Cooper brought out the idea of heat treatment on site as big vessels had to be taken to Darlington to a big furnace which was very costly. Coopers forsaw that whatever needed destressing could be performed on site, which would be more economical.

Destressing is required for anything that has been fabricated or where different parts have been welded together. There is always a lot of local stress when the welds cool off and very often they would fracture, so the idea was to heat up, as soon as the jobs were welded, to a given temperature and then cool down, doing away with all local stress. This turned out to be very big business.

Then Coopers acquired their first order which was to destress a vessel, which was a sphere made out of three inch thick steel plate weighing 50 tons. He made rough drawings and we made what they call a top hat furnace, made out of angle iron, a sort of square shed effect. Some wire meshing was placed over it and then three inch thick slabs of insulating materials fitted over the meshing, which had very good insulatory properties. A double layer of this was put on, which made it more of less fully insulated. There was very little heat lost and some of these channel heaters I have referred to were put around the base on the firebricks and then the 'top hat' was lifted and thermocouples were attached to different places on the sphere to record the heat to ensure it was heated uniformally. These were led out to an instrument called a recorder which recorded onto graphs exactly what was happening and when the job was finished the metallurgists evaluated the graph to check everything was right. The biggest electric furnace in the world was then made to destress vessels that weighed 350 tons.

The term vessel does not necessarily mean a ship, it can be anything in the form of a boiler, or whatever. These vessels weighed 350 tons and were to be destressed, so the furnace was made and numerous heaters were laid down either side of it. There was so much current required that they tapped straight onto the grid for it and when they were finally made they were floated out into the river and towed away to their destination. This was another highly successful job. We also made several different shapes of heaters, and did some jobs for one of the submarines to destress the ribs.

One day, an order came that the shipping repair dockyard wanted to heat a propellor belonging to a destroyer, but they were unable to remove it. It was suggested that they tried using some of our heaters, which they did and again that was a big saving. The heaters were placed around the propellor boss and covered in lagging and switched on, left for an hour or two and the boss was heated up. They were then able to draw the propellor off quite easily. We also got a big job in Wales. There was a 30-foot diameter pipe on one of the power stations and when they came to joint the final flanges the bolt holes were about three quarters of an inch out. It would have been an awful big job to have to cut and re-welded it, so instead we made some very long heaters. Three or four were placed around this pipe at a given place and lagged inside in order to contain the heat. They raised it to quite a good temperature and then by a system of winches, jacks and pulling devices they pulled the pipe over and were then able to connect it up with very little trouble.

Then came the biggest job of all – to destress the reactor at one of the major nuclear power stations which consisted of a large spider-like affair with several arms rotating from the centre and they had had numerous problems with the welds cracking. We were given several drawings and instructions on how to make up the heaters and a lot of frames had to be made of the same shape as the extended arms to fit over them. The same thing applied to the heaters, which were specially made and a lot of heat was required. There again, it was handy to tap straight into the grid, but nevertheless it was quite a job to fit all the heaters up. The job was ready to start and the structure was mounted on brick columns to keep it all in line. The people responsible wanted to know if these brick columns would support the weight which was, in fact, tremendous, so we had to do a test on these brick columns with over one hundred tons pressure, but of course, there were no presses about with that sort of testing power. It proved to be quite a successful test and they informed us that they wished to see this brick test under the actual conditions which would be heated from 700 to 800 degrees centigrade so then we had to put heaters around the column of bricks and there again cover it with insulation and leave the heat on overnight, but in order for us to do this we had to get an extra cable laid in at the works. The next morning they tested it for deflection and distortion but it proved to be that there was very little distortion or any untoward stresses so then the go-ahead was given to carry on with the job. In this connection I made a special crane to enable us to hoist all the section on to cover up this big application because it was quite difficult for men to handle them. I acquired a Ford 3-tonne crane which went up to quite a good height but it was fixed. There was no need to operate in any other way but hoisting so we had to get it tested by Weights and Measures which we did, and this test carried a certain weight and proved to be very satisfactory.

Coopers were quite a big concern by this time and were becoming known worldwide. Once we had made a furnace to ship to America and found out that there was to be a shipping strike in Hull the next day. We had a deadline to meet and a heavy penalty clause of £2,000 or £3,000 if the furnace was not delivered on time. We worked through the night and delivered it to Hull the evening before the dock strike was due to start. These things happen, of course!

We were getting so much work by this time that we decided to enlarge our premises. The plans were passed for the extensions but we left one part of the extension fairly high in order to lift up the sections because we needed headroom when we were building large furnaces.

During the period after the war, when I embarked on engineering projects at home, I bought, amongst other things five pedestal drilling machines. We collected these machines one at a time with the help of my boys. Some were incomplete, but I managed to make four good ones out of the five. When I got them home and came to take the first one to pieces, I found that it had a solid lead weight inside and at that time lead was bringing a very good price.

We were also able to make some very handy folding stools which we sold to various garden centres. We only ever had one complaint from a gentleman whose son had trapped his finger in one of the stools. He was very irate and I tried to explain to him that they worked on the same basis as a deck chair and care was needed when folding and unfolding them. However, after that we used screws with eyes on them so that they couldn't be collapsed without the hook and eye being undone.

Another time we bought hundreds of pieces of heavy plywood which we cut, shaped and screwed on mouldings to form a pattern. Eventually I used these to build a little wooden dog which we called Sniffer. It was a pull-along toy and when it was pulled along sandpaper, it sounded like a dog sniffing. We were able to sell quite a lot of these. They took several months to make but it all helped to educate our sons and kept me busy at night and weekends.

Before father disposed of his pantechnicon, I painted the inside with water paints, put in our double bed and some single beds for the boys, carpeted it, installed electric lights and off we went to Wales for our holidays. The boys had never been to the country before and I can just picture them now walking through the fields. The farmer supplied us with milk, butter, bread and home-cured bacon which we cooked for breakfast. The farmer and his family became very good friends of ours and we kept visiting them for many years. He had an accident one day when he was out shooting rabbits, the gun accidently went off and he lost a thumb. During the summer his wife used to take in visitors and looked after all the poultry and the milk round. They used to deliver milk to the town twice a day and had their own pony and cart for this purpose. I was so sorry when we lost touch with them.

Chapter Sixteen

Retiring to Anglesey farmwork

WHEN I finally retired at the age of 70 and left the running of the business entirely to my son, he more or less pensioned me off. My wife and I decided to move from the shop and house which we had in the town and went to look for another house. Quite by accident we came across a nice detached house in Liverpool Road, Ainsdale which was up for sale. We looked around and liked it immediately. The gardens and grounds and the whole fabric of the house appeared to be in excellent condition. We went to see the agents that same afternoon and bought it for £2,800. We moved in within a fortnight and I set to doing various alterations. We made two rooms into one and put in sliding doors. We stripped off all the wallpaper and painted everywhere a nice light colour. Eventually, we made it into two flats and found the rent from the other flat paid the mortgage. I built a sun lounge right across the back of the house, which was well over 30 feet long. I bought some T-irons and angles very cheaply, in fact I remember paying £7 for them. My intention was to use it as a sun lounge, but my wife had other ideas. She had it fully carpeted and curtained and made it into a nice lounge where we could hold parties. I even made a bar at one end and put up shelves for plants.

A little later on I made a couple of fish tanks and we had some lovely tropical fish. I was also very fond of birds so I cut a doorway in one end of the lounge and built an extension which took the form of an aviary. My wife was always afraid of mice getting into the house though and it worried her so much that I sold the birds and turned it into a billiards room, for which I made my own billiard table.

Then I built myself a garage and over the top I made what I called my play room. It was about 14 feet by 11 feet and I installed central heating and fitted the boiler. I made myself a nice model railway and used to spend a lot of time, not just playing with the trains but making scenery as well.

There was a workshop at the bottom of the garden and I bought several second-hand machines, mostly from London, including a milling machine with both horizontal and vertical heads, a shaping machine, a sheet metal folder, a power drill, an oxyacetylene and a welding set. I also bought an all-purpose woodworking machine which did sawing, planing, spindle moulding and drilling and at a later date I was able to purchase a band saw. I had no intention of just sitting with my feet up so I had the idea of making a steam engine. I had always had a fondness for steam and acquired drawings and bought castings. I began to machine everything up, it was a quarter scale, fully working, coal-fired steam tractor called Old Bill built on the lines of a 1903 Burrel tractor. Then I had the idea of making it into a fairground engine, which, of course, was more decorative and I made all the parts for it myself and in the end it was a fully-working fairground engine fitted on solid rubber tyres. I decided to make an organ to go with it, together with a set of gallopers. It would have made a unique combination, an engine, organ and a set of hobby horses. However, it was taking me such a long time to make the organ that I decided to start on the gallopers. I made one of the model horses which was about thirteen inches long. I went to Art School all through the winter months to make this model and I had intended to make 33 of them! I made up the organ which had flashing lights, dummy organ pipes and a very powerful amplifier. I also made a conductor who was very lifelike and a couple of dancing girls. Eventually I bought and overhauled a sixteen-foot caravan and I made one of the sides lift up and open and I mounted the traction engine and the organ inside. My intention was to utilise it to raise money for spastic children. I fitted a toilet inside and a cooking stove so that it was totally self-supporting.

Whichever property I acquired, my first priority was to dig a well in the garden so that we would always have a supply of water, especially when hosepipes were banned in summer. I dug a particularly large well as I intended making a pond over the top of the well and, while putting rubbish in the corner of the garden, I came across an old radiogram in which were nesting a family of baby robins with their mouths wide open. Naturally I left the nest there until they flew away.

One day I had a sprinkler going in the front garden when two young fellows walked past. They looked over the wall and told me I was not supposed to be using a hosepipe. I asked them why not and they said because there was a shortage of water. I told them that I had just spent three weeks of blood, sweat and tears digging the well from which the water was coming. They looked rather taken aback and apologised. Later I had a visit from a Water Board official to whom I had to explain the same thing – someone had seen me watering my garden and had reported me. He went away quite satisfied with my explanation and said that I would not be bothered again.

My son was carrying on the business very admirably at this time and it was expanding. I went round one morning to have a look and I saw a big pile of timber, which turned out to be brand new door frames which they were preparing to set fire to. I told him not to burn them and rushed home, got my trailer and took them back home with me. Eventually I obtained a circular saw and I was able to make several greenhouses out of this timber which I sold. I have always been a workaholic and get a great deal of satisfaction out of making things.

I made my wife a greenhouse for her house plants and I had my own, in which I grew flowers down one side, and cucumbers and tomatoes down the other.

My wife decided that it was about time we had a new car as I was still using the Hillman pick-up. I spoke to my sons and they said 'You can't take your money with you, go and buy yourself a new car'. Then they told me I could have a company car. I had never actually had a brand new car even though I had been driving since 1912 so I got in touch with the motor agents and they sent a salesman round to see me. I told him I wanted a car with a big engine and he suggested an Executive. He brought one round and it was a lovely car but it was an automatic which I didn't want, but he persuaded me to drive it and it was a very simple car to drive so I said I would have it. I paid £1,800 for it and the Hillman was taken in part exchange. I never regretted buying the Executive as my wife and I had some lovely outings and also at the same time we bought a caravan.

We eventually changed our fixed caravan up north for one in Wales where we had always spent our holidays. We bought a caravan on a site called Gorse Hill about two miles outside of Conway. We made friends with some people who lived in a residential caravan on the site. He was a retired chief engineer who had been all over the world and on Saturday evenings we would play cards and he would relate some of his experiences, but he would tell the same tale over and over again. The site was quite near to Llandudno and our wives would go and have a bingo session and we go would down to the pier and watch perhaps the Isle of Man ferry coming in. We were never bored as we both had hobbies – mine was drawing and painting and my wife's was embroidery.

I was reading the paper one morning when I saw a 'For Sale' advert for an 8-acre farm in Anglesey, with planning permission for eight caravans. I showed my wife and she was very interested as we had always wanted a farm. We went to have a look at it the same day, and although it had been rather neglected for some time the fabric of the house seemed good. Inside, the house was damp but we decided we liked it and it really was in a lovely setting in the middle of 8 acres with a disused quarry in one of the fields. We went to see the Agent and he told us the price was £5,500 – we offered him £5,000 cash and as the seller was ready to emigrate to Australia he accepted our offer.

We travelled from Conway every day while we were renovating the house and after a while we decided to sell the caravan and buy another one and place it on the farm site. We bought a fourteen foot long caravan with central heating installed and in no time it was placed on the farm site.

I wanted to get some capital coming in so I decided to develop the caravan site before we actually commenced work on the house. The field was uneven so I bought a bulldozer and a front loading digger and a back acter on the rear. I scooped out eight places for the caravans and then I applied for the mains to be put on. The authorities were not very helpful and kept me waiting over twelve months before they actually installed the cable.

I had to build a cesspool and armed with the diagrams I began to dig. I had not gone far when I hit solid rock, so I bought a ram and attached it to the bucket and tried to break the rock up but that did not work. I then got in touch with a contractor who came with a lot of heavy equipment which he fitted to his digger but even that did not work. He decided to blow it up but I was worried because it was very close to the village. However, he was also a councillor and he said it would be all right. They drilled holes and put in the charges and up it went, with rocks flying in the air.

I had a joiner helping me with the house and the biggest job was the removal of the floors which were full of dry rot. We concreted them throughout and covered them with bitumen before we put the carpets down. I put in new doorways and generally altered the inside of the house and made a porch on the outside. I also installed central heating and put in an extra toilet and shower downstairs. Eventually we were able to move in and the first thing we bought was a fridge/freezer, which enabled us to buy food in bulk for the many relatives and friends who we knew would be coming to visit.

I decided to move the caravan we had been living in to one of the sites and to also buy a new one. The new one had to be brought over the Menai Strait but the bridge was not wide enough to take a modern caravan of eight feet wide, so we ended up bringing it across on a pontoon, having hitched a motorboat onto the side of it and crossed the Strait that way. At the other side it was loaded onto a caravan transporter and taken to the site. We were charged an awful lot of money to do this, but it was the only way.

I sited the new caravan, fitted the water mains and then ran them to the sewer. I did not know whether I was going to light them by electricity or gas as at this time the cables still hadn't been installed. As a result of this I lost a whole year's rental on these two vans as they just stood idle. In the end I went down to the Electricity Board and explained my position. Four men duly arrived on the Monday morning, climbed up the post on the other side of the file and ran a cable down from their wires into my transformer. All this took two hours!

As it wasn't the caravan season, I decided to leave the wiring up and turn it into a garden centre and I built a shop just off the main road. I bought some secondhand trusses and set the framework up and one of my friends did the painting. I obtained several crates of glass and had it glazed but this gave us an awful lot of problems as there were eight gales in twelve months and the wind would whistle over the shop and sometimes it would blow the panes of glass out. If I had known this beforehand I would have used plastic sheeting. I bought the whole stock from a garden wholesaler who was selling the business, but told him I was short of capital and he arranged for us to repay him when I had sold the stock. We had problems at first, of course, especially when we bought the wrong compost for house plants and lost hundreds of plants. Later I built an extension to use for storing plants and also an unloading bay to cope with heavier items where I could draw up with my trailer.

My wife and I discussed the possibility of turning an old barn into a guest house and we asked a local surveyor to come and draw up some plans. He did not charge an awful lot of money and the idea was that we would cover over the yard between the barn and the house and make one large lounge with one side all glass, but it would have to have a flat roof. The plans were rejected because they said with the roof being flat it would not blend in with the surrounding countryside, which I thought was quite ridiculous.

By this time we had ten grandchildren who were all growing up and we were hardly seeing enough of them. It was such a long journey, about four and a half hours in a car. We put the farm up for sale and soon an American gentleman came along and decided to buy it. He asked if he could come and live in the caravan with his wife while he was waiting for the some deeds to come through from America and we agreed.

We were very reluctant to leave the farm as we had made some very nice friends and were looked upon by most people as country squires. However, the three main reasons we were leaving were lack of working capital, missing our grandchildren and the fact that if either of us were taken ill, the nearest hospital was at Bangor twelve miles away.

During the time we lived on the farm we had all the benefits of fresh air and the satisfaction of having owned our own farm and we felt rather sad when we were leaving. Fortunatley we had kept our house in Ainsdale so there was no hardship in having to move. We had worked awfully hard on the farm and we came out with exactly what we had put in.

Chapter Seventeen

A mournful return to Southport

WE soon settled back in our home and, of course, I looked for something to do as usual. I carried on making greenhouses, sheds and numerous other items. Then one day my wife and I were passing the local aerodrome and I said to her, 'I think I'll have some flying lessons!' I had always wanted to fly and had never had a real opportunity after having been refused by the RFC in 1917. I asked her if she would mind if I had some flying lessons. 'No, not really, if you would like it, go ahead.' So I went straight away and booked the lessons.

I was 74 when I had my first lesson, at Woodvale. The Chief Instructor took me up, and it turned out to be quite stormy and as we climbed higher it began to rain quite heavily. We were being buffetted about and I was beginning to feel quite sick having previously had a good breakfast. The instructor said, 'Oh, just relax Mr Manning, just look for your house.' This, of course, was to distract me. I was unable to see my house at that time because of the trees, but I felt too ill to look for anything and thought to myself, 'Oh, I hope I'm not going to be sick.' Luckily I wasn't.

I enjoyed the flying lessons and one morning I went up with the instructor and I said, 'Sometime would you like to go over Anglesey, I would love to take a photograph of the old farm.' 'Oh yes, I like going along that coast, there are plenty of places for a forced landing,' he said.

I did not think that was a very good thing to say to a student pilot. My flying lessons were cut short due to the fact that I caught pneumonia. I had always been as fit as a fiddle but I was quite poorly. In fact I had twenty-one injections and I would often say to the nurse, 'Are you making a pattern and are there many spaces left?'. She would laugh and say, 'I'll find enough spaces don't you worry about it!' However, I soon recovered and was back on my feet again.

My wife was very fond of embroidery and in fact she attended a class for many years. It was a type of social meeting and quite a number of ladies attended on one afternoon a week. She was able to learn the finer points of needlework and she embroidered a beautiful table cloth, for which she received the first prize of a silver cup in a competition. I have since given this table cloth to one of my grand-daughters and I know she treasures it.

She was also very fond of flower arranging and she had classes for this as well. She exhibited at the Southport Flower Show and I used to go with her the night before and we would practically spend all the evening arranging the flowers.

One year I had the idea of making a miniature cottage and garden with a waterfall, a pond, and real stone walls. I even made real wrought-iron gates and was able to get hold of some small plants and shrubs to make a rockery and I was quite pleased with the outcome. One year I won a prize for the best cactus in the Show, and after the event a gentleman came up to me and asked me if I would be prepared to sell him the cactus and he offered me £3.00 for it. Apparently he had a friend, who was also a competitor and lived down the road, and this man wanted to buy my cactus to be able to put it in his greenhouse to show his friend up. However, I did not let him have it because it was quite valuable.

It took me ten years to build the steam engine mentioned earlier, but it was very satisfying work and I donated it to the Imperial Cancer Research Fund and it is now based at Chester. It goes out periodically fund raising and makes quite a lot of money for the Fund.

I also decided to build a swimming pool. My wife did not want me to as she thought that the work would be too strenuous for me. I dug a hole outside the sun lounge and positioned one of the wagons from the works down the entry, then I ran a plank up from the floor into the body of the wagon to dispose of the soil. I spent about three weeks digging this hole which was about fifteen feet by nine feet by three feet deep. When I had finished digging the hole I asked my son, who had a bricklayer and a labourer working for him on his furnace, if he would let them come and put the base in for me.

I would not have been able to do this myself in one day, so they came and they did it for me. They put a six inch layer of concrete down and smoothed it all and then I began to build up the sides and then I plastered them. I made my own plaster and placed a surround along the top and handrails.

I obtained hardwood rails and made brackets and fixed them on. I made an outlet and an inlet and then I gave it three coats of waterproof paint which in fact was quite expensive. I then let it dry and eventually I was in a position to fill it with water. But I was very disappointed because several bubbles appeared in the plaster so I had to empty out all the water. Dark patches appeared in the plaster where the bubbles had been. I repainted it and filled it up with water again hoping that this time I would be more successful. It was not to be, exactly the same thing happened, the bubbles appeared again. I just did not know what to do next.

I made contact with some people who were advertising plastic pool liners at a reasonable price. I measured the pool and sent them the dimensions. When the liner arrived it wasn't a very good fit but I decided to take a chance and filled it up with water.

Occasionally air would get underneath between the plastic sheeting and the base and it felt like you were walking on air. I decided to insert a piece of piping down between the sheeting and the side of the pool and was able to pump out the air and the condensation.

My ten grandchildren would come to visit us and we really had a lot of fun with this pool, especially during the summer months. In the winter I decided to cover it over so I bought some bed irons very cheaply and made a structure from the sun lounge. I made a continuous roof and covered it with plastic corrugated sheeting. I then installed radiators which were fed from the house hot water system. I tried heating the water in the pool by a domestic boiler which I had purchased quite reasonably but it wasn't very successful as it took an awful long time to heat up the water. It was very disappointing having to wait for the water to become warm enough to dive into.

I had seen an advert for a Canadian boiler and I eventually purchased one of these. It had a new stainless steel system of jets and was constructed out of brass. It was expensive to purchase but it was quite economical to run. It meant that every morning before breakfast I was able to jump straight out of bed and into the pool.

One day I went to visit my doctor and I asked him if he'd been swimming at 8 o'clock this morning and he replied 'No, but I don't suppose you brought a baby into the world at 2 o'clock this morning, did you?'

After a while my wife decided that she would like to live in a bungalow. I liked the idea and, of course, by this time I was getting itchy feet and wanted to move and develop another house. So we decided to look around. We saw a bungalow in Liverpool Road, Birkdale, which was up for sale so we went and asked if we could have a look around and eventually bought it. When we moved in I had quite a lot of timber left over from the days when I made the greenhouses and also I did not have anywhere to put the machinery so I sold it to different model makers.

There had been a summer house attached to the back of the house which had been used as a kitchen, but there wasn't very much room. I asked a surveyor to come and draw up some plans for a kitchen extension. The plans were passed and I moved the summer house to the bottom of the garden and we were then able to sit in it and view the lovely garden which we had.

We had quite a big front garden with double drive gates but the wall had a bad slant to it and looked as if it would collapse at any time. I completely demolished it and put a concrete footing down the whole length. I also built a wall and made some new gates.

Whilst I was building this wall a gentleman stopped his car and came across to me and said, 'Would you like to give me a price for my wall to be redone?' So I told him that I was very sorry, but this was just a hobby of mine and that I lived there. Nevertheless he told me that I was making a very good job of it. I also made a car port and it was a pleasure to come home on a cold, wet night and be able to get out of the car in the dry and go straight into the house. I walled off a section of the garden at the bottom to use a a kitchen garden. I planted several different fruit trees and several different varieties of grapevines.

I decided that I would like to do some woodwork again so I purchased some more woodworking machinery. I also began making a grandfather clock and a china cabinet out of solid mahogany. I made the mouldings and I bought a machine which I had seen advertised to make the spiral columns. For the grandfather clock I bought a German movement with full Westminster chimes and made some working blacksmiths to place over the top of the clock. The figures were just over three inches tall and the blacksmith on the right hand side used one hammer to strike the anvil on every quarter and the other side was a striker with a big hammer to strike the anvil on the hour. I encountered considerable difficulties when making the striker because both hands had to be on the hammer shaft and also it had to be frictionless. Eventually after a lot of experimenting I was able to get them to work perfectly. They were real blacksmiths with caps and a beard and sleeves rolled up and wearing leather aprons and were painted authentically. I made a forge in the background consisting of a smithy wall with various tools hanging on the wall. My eldest son now has this clock and it stands in his hall and has been working for the last five years.

We celebrated our fiftieth wedding anniversary soon after we had finished the alterations to the house and we entertained quite a number of people. We had some visitors from America – my wife's relations – and although she had never met them before she had communicated with them for several years. We went to meet them at Manchester Airport and the plane was late. We had to stand and wait in the cold for quite sometime and as a result of this she developed a very bad cough and cold. The doctor prescribed antibiotics, but unfortunately they did not do the job.

We went to the doctor's again and he wanted her to go and have an x-ray but she wouldn't go. Eventually, the doctor insisted that she went and had it. The consultant came along and said that he would like her to have a scan. However, instead of having a scan she went into hospital for three days and he took a sample from her lungs and then came the terrible news that she had lung cancer. This was the worst episode of my whole life.

When I went to visit her that same evening with one of my sons who is a doctor, the consultant called us to one side and asked us how we were going to tell her. I told him that she had always been so very clean in every possible way and had looked after herself tremendously all of her life. She had never smoked and I thought that if I told her that she had cancer she would immediately feel very dirty but the consultant said that we would have to tell her.

My son actually wanted to tell her but I didn't like the idea of telling her this, because I knew what a terible shock it would be for her. However, we continued to attend the clinic and each time she had to have an x-ray.

I could see the black shape growing bigger and bigger and I was terribly upset. Eventually the consultant decided that she should have some special treatment and he informed us that a friend of his was using some new capsules and that they were giving good results. He placed her on these, but unfortunately, they had a very bad side effect. She had had a beautiful head of hair all her life and as a result of taking these capsules she lost every bit of her hair, which was extremely sad. I bought her a wig for when we went out but she was terribly unhappy about this.

On one occasion when we went to the clinic the consultant was away and one of his assistants saw us. He told us that he thought that there had been some improvement. This news bucked us up, of course, but he was only trying to get out of an awkward situation.

She eventually became very ill and in the end we had to bring in a day nurse and a night nurse to look after her.

Sometimes I could see her silently crying, but she never complained. One day she said to me, 'I'm not going to get better, am I?' 'Oh well,' I said, 'you mustn't give up hope, I'm praying for a miracle to happen and miracles do happen.'

My son did not have a lot of hope and he didn't recommend that she have an operation. He said that I must take her out and do whatever I could for her.

We used to go out in the car every day and we would go on picnics but eventually she became too ill to go out. I asked my sons if they thought that she would get better attention in a nursing home, even though I did not like the idea of her going in. They all decided, especially my son who is a doctor, that this would be the best thing for her because she would receive all the attention necessary, including oxygen as she was also having great difficulty in breathing. The doctor arranged for her to go into a nursing home and my youngest son and his wife took her in one morning. It was a terrible thing for me, seeing her drive away.

Sadly, she was only in the nursing home three days before she died. This was a terribly upsetting time for me. I had been looking after her from June and it was now November. It was very sad knowing that one day it would happen but I used to pray for a miracle.

I had always had the idea that if she had had a scan or if cancer had been diagnosed sooner then she may possibly still be with me today. When I told my son of my feelings he said, 'Try not to think of it in that way Dad, because it quite likely would have been too late to have taken any active treatment.'

I decided to continue living by myself in the bungalow, even for the very night of the funeral. I was quite determined that I would have to face the future. I always felt her presence in this particular bungalow and I was never frightened of being on my own. I lived there for 18 months and I used to do all my own cooking and washing and my relations would come to visit me.

In the meantime I decided to work for the Cancer Research Fund and I got out my engine and organ and purchased a second-hand 16 foot caravan and mounted the engine and the organ in it. I contacted the Cancer Research Fund and enquired if they would like to accept this as a fund raiser. The area manager came to my house and he arranged for the committee, which was based in Chester, to come to see me. Six of them came one day and they called themselves Chester Friends of the Imperial Cancer Research Fund. As soon as they saw the engine they were really pleased with the idea. They came for it the following Saturday and took it away.

I felt very sad really when I saw it going away after having spent ten years making it, but I knew that it would do a lot for cancer research. In fact on one afternoon alone it raised as much as £2,500. It has been used for collections in numerous counties and various rallies all over the country, and I know that this is all due to my dear wife. She told me a long time ago not to sell it and if she only knew the good it is doing for cancer research I know that she would be very happy.

My son progressed and expanded the business by leaps and bounds but then unfortunately he struck a bad patch. A firm owed him an awful lot of money and there were court proceedings. It was a very distressing time for him. Now he has made a great success of it after having had many setbacks. After I had disposed of the organ to Cancer Research, I would go to the works and help him out. I would start mid-morning and have my lunch there. Actually he let me have a little shed in one of the big workshops and I would sit in it and have my lunch. He also knew that I liked a nap after my lunch. I would work until perhaps four o'clock and go home before dark. I thoroughly enjoyed this because I knew that in a way I was helping him and, of course, it was providing me with something to do. One Monday morning I set off to go to the works and my left eye seemed very strange. I could not see very well and when I arrived at the works I told by son that I could not see very well out of my left eye. He said that he thought that it would get better very soon. I managed to drive the car for the rest of that week with my one good eye and then on the Saturday morning my other eye went exactly the same as the left, and it just wasn't safe for me to drive.

I went to see my doctor and he arranged for me to go and see an eye specialist. I went to see one and he looked into both of my eyes and then said that I had lost three-quarters of the sight in both eyes. Of course this was a terrible shock and when he said he wanted me to go to see a physician this is what I immediately did. The physician examined me and said that he wanted me to have a brain scan, so one of my grandsons took me to Walton Hospiotal. In the scanner room the doctor asked me to lie down and as I suffer from claustrophobia I did not like the idea of having to lie flat on my back. He set the machine going and then went into a room to install the film. 'Every minute you'll feel a movement,' he said. It was a sort of tunnel, and I remember thinking to myself 'I hope it moves outwards instead of inwards.' The machine made a most peculiar clanking noise, almost like a washing machine and it seemed an awfully long time before he eventually switched it off. Then he gave me an injection and repeated the process all over again. He asked me if I would like to have a look at the picture, but I told him that I did not particularly want to see my brain on film.

He said that he would be sending a letter to the physician who subsequently informed me that there were no growths of my brain, and that it had evidently been a blockage of one of the small arteries which clogged the optical nerve. Later on, my son told me that I was rather unfortunate in having both eyes affected, because the optical nerve is fed through a Y-shaped system of arteries and it is usually only one of the top parts of the Y that become blocked, but in my case it was the bottom part of the Y that had become blocked thereby causing tunnel vision. Fortunately for me, I wasn't totally blind, but I was not able to see well enough to enable be to carry on driving the car. This was rather sad as I had held a driving licence for well over seventy-one years. Naturally, I had to be taken everywhere and sadly I had to dispose of my car. It was a very traumatic experience for me so soon after having lost my dear wife. I had to have extra lights in my room which I would leave on all the time. One night I woke up having gone to sleep as I always did with the lights on, and it was pitch black. I had this terrifying thought of having gone totally blind, it was really frightening and I prayed that this hadn't happened. I reached out for my lamp and switched it on and sure enough I could see the light. It was only the bulb that had gone.

One day I was driving with my elder son and I said to him, 'Well, there's not much to live for, I don't mind whether I live or die, I can't look forward to anything, I can't appreciate beauty in any shape or form and I can't make any plans.' But my son said, 'Well you do have something to look forward to, you still have your family, you have your ten grandchildren and you can watch their progress and you can still help by making things, can't you?' 'Yes, I suppose I can.' I said.

I was really very depressed, but I think it was because of the tablets which the doctor had given to me in an endeavour to correct the blood condition I had. If fact, I became very ill, but after talking with my son I began to feel much better and stopped feeling sorry for myself. I took on a new lease of life and started to make things for cancer research.

In the meantime my family thought that I should not be living on my own, and my younger son suggested that I should go and live with him. He had a big garage alongside his bungalow and said that if he demolished this he would be able to build me a grandad flat. Needless to say, I did not like the idea at first, but eventually I moved in and, in fact, I was quite happy there.

I had a workshop and a greenhouse, but I hadn't been there very long when my son decided to move. He bought a two-acre plot of land and obtained planning permission to build a detached house which incorporated a grandad flat for me. Again, I had a huge greenhouse and workshop but I couldn't see well enough to look after them, so eventually I gave up my greenhouse, which was very sad as I was fond of growing flowers and plants.

Before I became ill, I had bought a couple of steam locomotives and my intentions were to make a garden railway for the younger children to drive around the garden. I managed to take one of them to pieces, but the other one was brand new and needed finishing off. One of my sons acquired for me a lathe and several other machines. However, I found that I just could not see well enough to carry on, although I think now that if I had made a determined effort I could have managed it.

At this time my middle son who had the business would pick me up each day after lunch and take me down to the works. He fitted me out with a couple of benches and some powerful overhead lights and a band saw, a finishing machine, a circular saw and planer, all of which I had to use with great care.

I also thought that I would like to make another organ as I had been making smaller items such as bird feeding trays, tom-tit boxes and plant stands. I began making the organ which was to take the form of a street piano organ. Firstly, I made the ornamental wheels, springs and axle and then I made the body of the piano. I had the idea of trying to incorporate a toy monkey into it, so after numerous advertisements I was able to obtain a lovely model of a small chimpanzee. I decided to make him rise out of the roof of the organ when the handle was turned and gyrate a little, and then go slowly out of sight again. I got a piece of one-inch stainless steel tubing and made a piston and a long rod which projected through the top of the organ. Then I tried various means of generating compressed air to force this piston up the tube and eventually I hit on the idea of using one of the old-fashioned type pumps, where you had to put your foot on the base and pump it up and down with the handle. I made a simple mechanism to work on the pulley and belt system, so that when you turned the handle it also worked a crank which lifted the piston up and down.

Then I bought a second-hand windscreen wiper motor to make the monkey revolve but I found this task very difficult to perform and, in the end, used the mechanism from the wiper motor which was on a crank and made suitable connections to the monkey which made him rock to and fro. The monkey had a red pork-pie hat and a red jacket.

I fitted a very powerful amplifier and decorated it very nicely, and placed a sign on the top which could be lowered and laid down flat. It had a couple of shafts which the normal authentic street organs had to enable them to be pushed around the streets. Unfortunately, it only had ornamental wheels and if it were to be pushed along rough roads it would soon collapse, so I decided to make a trailer and picked up a rear axle, complete with springs, wheels and tyres from a scrapyard.

I began making the chassis, but I was unable to see to use the electric welder and had to get one of the lads from the works to do the welding for me. The chassis was finished and I made the van body which was tall and narrow, and the backboard I used as a ramp, so that the organ could be pulled out of the trailer. Finally I fitted lights and indicators and painted it.

I approached the area manager of the Imperial Cancer Research Fund and told him that I had already donated an organ and would they like to have the new one which I had made. He paid me a visit and told me that he was very interested indeed and that he would come back for it soon. He had a towing hook fitted to his car and came for the organ which he took to Manchester where it is based. Personally, I derive tremendous satisfaction knowing that it was my idea, and that I had made it out of very simple components. There is very little maintance required, possibly a spot of oil evey now and then on the cross shafts.

The tapes which it plays are all authentic street piano or street organ music and also, the fact that I installed dummy organ pipes, completes the illusion.

I still miss my wife terribly. It takes a bit of getting used to after over sixty years together. I have an enlarged picture of her in my room which one of my nieces presented to us on our 50th wedding anniversary. She is always smiling down and sometimes when I an doing my daily exercises, I often say to her, 'Aye, it's alright for you to sit there laughing at me. Here I am having to do all these hard exercises to keep me going.' She really was a wonderful person.

After the organ had gone I continued to make the rocking horses. I had previously made some for the Imperial Cancer Research Fund who would raffle them, or sell them in their shops. In fact, one of my rocking horses raised £640. To date, I have made nearly one hundred and they are suitable for children up to the age of eight or nine. I am sure that they will last for generations because they are so well made.

I was not going to make any more but a lady came round a while ago and said that I had promised her one. She had lost my telephone number so she came to the works to remind me. Apparently she was the chaiman of a group of churches and they held fund-raising events to help old people. Being elderly myself and living with old people I was quite prepared to help. I just had one rocking horse left and she came with her husband, put the rocking horse in the car, and hoped to raise a lot of money with it.

I decided at this time to try and make another six rocking horses before Christmas 1987. In the meantime I met a gentleman who said that he had read an article in the newspaper that I was going to make rocking horses for cancer research. He told me that he had a set of woodworking machinery and that he would be able to cut out and machine the items for me. I accepted, and he said that he would keep in touch with me. With this in mind I thought that I would be able to make a lot more, so I decided on twenty. My son ordered the wood and other parts and I cut the wood ready to the required lengths. I then saw the man concerning the machinery and he informed me that due to ill health he had to sell the machinery and therefore was not in a position to help me. This meant that I had all this wood which was of no use for any other purpose, so I set to in April, 1987 and I managed to finish them in time for Christmas. It was a colossal job but I am happy knowing now how much they will make for charity.

Whilst I was in the process of making the rocking horses I was informed of a happy event. One of my grand-daughters has given birth to a beautiful baby girl, so that now makes me a great-grandad.

In between times I was making plant stands, bird boxes and bird feeding tables. I decided to try and make a better quality of plant stand, so instead of painting them I an now varnishing them. As a matter of fact, I find varnishing the natural wood far easier than having to give it two or three coats of paint. I make one type which stands on its legs for the hall, and another which screws on to the wall. I also made a wall clock for my middle son with full Westminster chimes. I managed to make the cabinet but I was not too happy with it as I was unable to get the corners right. My son has told me that he will finish it off for me. I have also made a grandfather clock for my grandson, who recently qualified as a vet.

I decided that I would like to make another organ, so I told my son and he agreed that it would be a good idea. He is very good, he supplies me with all the wood and materials. I had thought of incorporating one of my rocking horses into it as I felt that this would attract attention. I acquired some fairly heavy wheels with pneumatic tyres and made the axle and springs and completed it with two handles and legs. I then made the body and put a folding sign on the top of it and mounted a rocking horse. I installed a crank, which when you turned the handle rocked the horse. I managed to obtain another monkey and fitted it securely onto the rocking horse's back. I then put some real organ pipes round and fitted an amplifier so that when you turned the handle it switched the music on.

When it was finished I approached the local paper to see if they could get somebody to work it over the Christmas period, but I didn't get any volunteers, which was very sad. It just stood in the works over Christmas whereas it could have been making money. In the end the Imperial Cancer Research Fund put out enquiries and the Scottish area representative was very interested in taking over the organ and my son arranged for it to be delivered to Scotland. They are delighted with it and are in the process of having it painted, decorated and lettered before it starts its official duties in Scotland. They also took several of my bird boxes and sent me a lovely letter to say that they were selling very well and quite recently I received another letter to say that the organ is now doing well, too.

Whilst my grandson, who has now qualified as a veterinary surgeon was studying at Liverpool University, my middle son asked me if I would like to go with them to see him. Unfortunately, it was one of the days when I could not see very well. The university is set in beautiful surroundings and my grandson showed us around. He showed us where they perform the operations of the horses and cattle.

They had a large hydraulic table and an overhead electric hoist, which when the operation had been completed transported the animal into the recovery room next door. The room was padded because when the animals are coming out of the anaesthetic they tend to get a bit rough and could do harm to themselves. We saw a sheep which had given birth to twins but couldn't stand up or feed them, so the surgeon had made artificial legs for it to help it stand upright until it got the use in its own legs back. We also saw a horse which had had an operation on its eye which was removed because of an infection. I told them that when I worked in the smithy we had a horse called Johnny One-Eye who had lost his eye on some barbed wire but still used to go trotting around the yard.

My son took us all out for a most enjoyable meal and afterwards we went back to the veterinary school where my grandson showed us his living quarters. They were beautifully made and very modern. I am quite sure that he will make a very good vet. He is very kind and, in fact, when has has to put an animal down he always says a little prayer.

I am very thankful that I am still able to get about, even though it is very frustrating crossing roads. I manage to walk three or four miles every morning, wet or fine, snow or fog, and intend to keep up these exercises for as long as I am able. I always carry my white stick although at first I was rather embarrassed about holding it out when I wanted to cross the road. People do not realise what a shock it is to someone who can hardly see to have to try and cross the road, especially when a car comes past and accelerates – you have no idea whether to speed up your pace or stop. I wrote to the local paper asking them if they would print an article asking motorists to give a little thought to elderly or blind persons trying the cross the road.

My mother was 82 when she died. She had a stroke and went into a coma one Saturday night and was still in a coma on the following Thursday. She was very strong and kept trying to get up and I spent most of the four days and nights holding her down on the bed, but sadly she died. My mother and father were a grand couple and I have very happy memories of them. I am thankful for the way in which they brought our family up. They never had a lot of money but they gave us the best possible attention and put us on the right road. They both died very happy and when I think back I feel tremendously proud of them.

Quite recently I went to have my travelpass renewed. I haven't been very confident about travelling by bus for the last few years because one of the most awkward things when you can't see very well is keeping the drivers waiting whilst you fumble about for change. So, having acquired my pass I decided to put it to the test. I feel quite guilty having to ask people to take me everywhere, so I plucked up the courage to find my way to the station. Eventually, the train from Liverpool arrived, but it was pretty full so I stood in the doorway. Just before we set off a lady came in, stood next to me and asked me if I was alright. I said that I was and she was very friendly and on arrival at Southport she helped me off as she could see that I was a little confused. People were everywhere and although I thought that I knew Southport station well and even though the shop was just outside the station precinct, I was still utterly confused. The lady said 'I hope you will not think me too familiar if I suggest that I take you to the shop to which you want to go.' I told her that I would be very pleased indeed. She took my arm and I went into the shop and made my purchase. When we came out she said that she would take me back to the barrier. The day had brightened so much it was difficult for me to see. We had a nice conversation and she told me that she had been in the hospital service for a number of years and that her husband had been a prisoner-of-war in Japan for three years. He now helps out at the British Red Cross shop three days a week to help repay all the Red Cross did for him when he was an prisoner. It is nice when you come across someone like this lady. When the time came for me to catch the train back home I showed my pass to the ticket collector, and asked him if I could use it on a Sunday and he replied, 'You can use it on anything but Concorde.' I said 'That's a pity, because I would really love to go to America.'

My middle son has expanded the business so much since my retirement that he now exports all over the world. His youngest son who finished at college this year carried out some of his practical course work with his father. He is a great help to him both technically and practically and is adapting himself very well into the business. He seems to have inherited the Manning traits of perseverance, accuracy and effectiveness. He is the fourth generation, and I am quite sure that he is going to make an excellent engineer. I also think that he has some of his grandfather's qualities and believes in the old adage my father used to say, 'There's no use crying over spilt milk, let's get on with it.' This is also my son's attitude as he has had quite a lot of setbacks and has come through them.

I am very proud of the way in which my son has progressed and it gives me great pleasure when I often sit in the car waiting for him to take me home after I have been to the works for the afternoon, to see the staff coming to and fro and to hear the telephones ringing. I am quite sure that his grandfather would have been very proud and pleased to see this set-up. My son now has one of the biggest furnaces in the north of England for heat treatment. I am sorry that I am unable to see what is going on and I sometimes have to ask the men what they are making or what they are doing, because I am still very interested but, of course, a lot of it is beyond my comprehension.

To think that it all started with my father working as an apprentice in the pitsaw over one hundred years ago and the firm has always had a good name as far as integrity and for playing the game the way it should be played. I am very proud of my family and I now have ten grandchildren, the youngest being fourteen. She seems to be getting on well at school and enjoys the school work. She has a lovely singing voice and is also learning to play the harp. I am very fortunate to have such a good family whom I regularly visit and as previously mentioned I now have two great-granddaughters .

In my prayers at night I ask the good Lord, amongst other things to let me keep the remainder of my sight so that I can still go on making things and helping people, which in fact, occupies most of my time. I never become bored, perhaps sometimes a little depressed, but I am a firm believer in meditation. If I am unable to sleep of feel agitated I meditate for about half an hour. I never take sleeping tablets because I find meditation helps me to relax and this enables me to sleep well.

There are eighteen elderly ladies in the home where I live with my youngest son and his wife. Two of the ladies are immobile and most are disabled in one way or another. Very often I will go into the lounge and try to cheer them up. They look forward to listening to my various tales and they follow my progress with interest. There is one dear, old lady in particular who has suffered from arthritis for the past twenty years. She has an artificial hip and she is nearly always in pain, but she is so cheerful and always has a happy smiling face. She is a credit to us all and you never hear her complain.

I am now 90 and, if the good Lord will allow me, I am hoping to donate most of the proceeds of this book, if it should be a success, towards research into the causes and possible cures for cancer.

I am coming to the end of my story and I hope you have enjoyed some of the things I have written about. I think in an autobiography one ought to relate things as they happened. I do hope that none of the things that I have written about prove to be offensive in any shape or form as it is not my intention.

At last I must end my writings after three years. I have been asked on several occasions 'Were they good old days?' and now you have read it all. I have tried to relate everything as it happened without being boastful or conceited and hope that I have been successful. I am sure older readers will enjoy the nostalgia and say, 'I remember that'. and that younger readers will say, 'Fancy living like that.' There will be morals to study and help them be more satisfied with present day conditions.

I hope that there will be a huge demand for the book at home and abroad and that the cause of combating cancer will benefit considerably.

THE END

Note on the illustrations

MOST of the illustrations used in this book are from the author's own collection. We would like to thank the Trustees of the Science Museum in London, however, for their particular kindness in allowing us to reproduce many fascinating photographs from their collection free of charge. These add considerably to the interest of the book and illustrate well many of the technical advances and changes with which our family were so fully involved over many years.

Where the exact provenance of photographs is not known, we have made every effort to find out in whom copyright resides in these cases. We apologise if we have omitted to acknowledge copyright owners where these could not be traced.